Office 2000

Manon Cassade

An imprint of PEARSON EDUCATION

PEARSON EDUCATION LIMITED

Head Office:
Edinburgh Gate
Harlow
Essex CM20 2JE
Tel: +44 (0)1279 623623
Fax: +44 (0)1279 431059

London Office:
128 Long Acre
London WC2E 9AN
Tel: +44 (0)207 447 2000
Fax: +44 (0)207 240 5771

First published in Great Britain 2000

© Pearson Education Limited 2000

First published in 1999 as
Se Former En Un Jour: Office 2000
by Simon & Schuster Macmillan (France)
19, rue Michel Le Comte
75003 Paris
France

Library of Congress Cataloging in Publication Data
Available from the publisher.

British Library Cataloguing in Publication Data
A CIP catalogue record for this book can be obtained from the British Library.

ISBN 0-13-016228-0

All rights reserved. No part of this publication may be reproduced, stored in a retrieval system, or transmitted, in any form, or by any means, electronic, mechanical, photocopying, recording or otherwise, without prior permission, in writing, from the publisher.

10 9 8 7 6 5 4 3 2 1

Translated and typeset by Cybertechnics, Sheffield.
Printed and bound in Great Britain by Ashford Colour Press, Gosport, Hampshire.

The publishers' policy is to use paper manufactured from sustainable forests.

Contents

Introduction

Office 2000 comes to you with many enhancements and improvements. Among the most important ones, we will mention higher stability, a better response to users' needs (the environment responds to your actions), and increased integration with the Internet, with new functionalities to publish on the Web, navigate, and so on.

This book will help you to become acquainted with Office 2000 and to discover all the new features that have been introduced. Whether you are a beginner or an expert user, this book is meant for you, because it explains all the procedures proposed by Microsoft for you to be able to work quickly and easily. It also suggests expert tips and tricks to improve your performance.

How do I use this book?

Since chapters are independent of each other, you can read them in the order you choose. To find a command quickly, consult the index at the end of the book. It will help you to move more quickly through the topics. The book is structured as follows:

- Chapters 1 and 2 are a quick introduction to Office 2000. You will discover the various interface features as well as the commands which are shared by all the applications: opening a file, saving, and so on.

- Chapters 3 and 4 teach you how to use indispensable Word functions.
- Chapters 5 and 6 explain how to become the king of calculations with Excel.
- Chapters 7 and 8 are dedicated to creating presentations with PowerPoint.
- Chapters 9 and 10 deal with Outlook.
- Chapters 11 and 12 will make a perfect typesetter out of you, thanks to Publisher.

Adopted conventions

Please note that all commands are displayed in bold. Throughout the text, a number of symbols will alert you to a terminology issue, a technical detail, or indicate shortcuts or advice to the user. You will find three types of symbols:

Here you will find additional information.

This symbol warns you about problems you may encounter in certain cases. It also warns you what not to do. If you follow the instructions, you should not have any problems.

This symbol provides you with suggestions and tips: keyboard shortcuts, advanced techniques, and so on.

This icon shown on the margin of paragraphs marks Office 2000 new features.

1 Help, checks and Web tools

Office Assistant:
an effective and attentive help

Help

Wizards and templates

Spelling and Grammar check

Find and Replace

Office 2000 and the Web

In this first chapter, we will be studying the various procedures you need to follow to get Help. We will also be looking at all the tools for speeding up work, checking spelling, grammar, and so on and you will find a detailed description of all the functionalities of Office 2000.

The functions you are going to discover in this chapter are shared by all Office applications.

■ Office Assistant: an effective and attentive help

Introduced with Office 97, the Office Assistant takes you through all operations. If you are not familiar with version 97, the Office Assistant is a little paper clip which works very hard to provide advice when you need it. A faithful, effective and competent Assistant, it never fails you.

When you launch an Office application, the Office Assistant is activated by default (see Figure 1.1).

*If, when you launch the application, the Office Assistant does not come up, click on the **Help for Microsoft Name of application** button in the Standard toolbar in the active application.*

To ask the Office Assistant a question, click on it. Type the question in the text area (see Figure 1.2), then click on **Search**. A list of icons is displayed: click on the one that corresponds to your search. If the list of icons is not relevant, click on **Next** to display the follow-up.

For some tasks, the Office Assistant may offer its help of its own accord. In this case it displays a text balloon. Click on the Assistant to view its advice.

To hide the Office Assistant, click on ? (question mark) in the Menu bar, then select **Hide Office Assistant**.

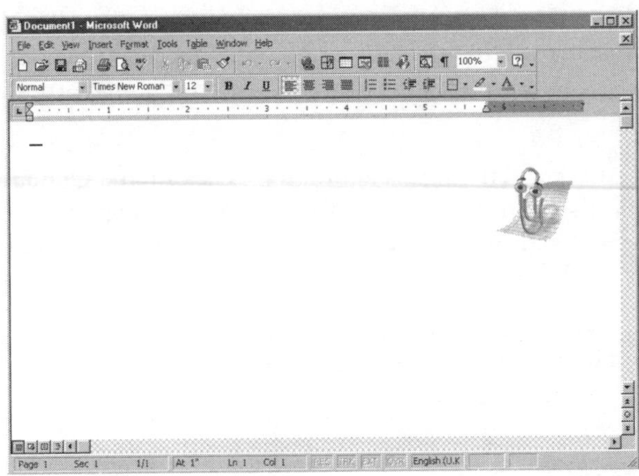

Figure 1.1 As soon as you start an application, the Office Assistant is displayed.

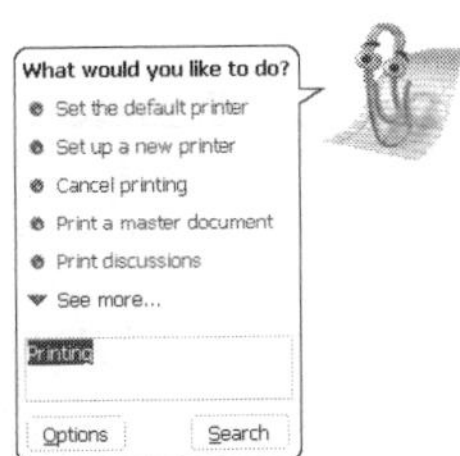

Figure 1.2 Ask the Office Assistant a question.

Office Assistant options

You can modify the Office Assistant default options, for example, you can choose a different look:

1. Click with the right mouse button (right-click), then select **Choose Assistant.**
2. Click on the **Gallery** tab. Scroll through the various types of Assistants by clicking on the **Next** button or the **Back**

button. The display area shows the 'face' of the selected Assistant.

3. Once you have specified your choice, click on **OK** to confirm.

To modify the Office Assistant options, click on the **Options** tab in the Office Assistant dialog box (see Figure 1.3). Activate/deactivate the options you require or do not require. Click on **OK** to confirm.

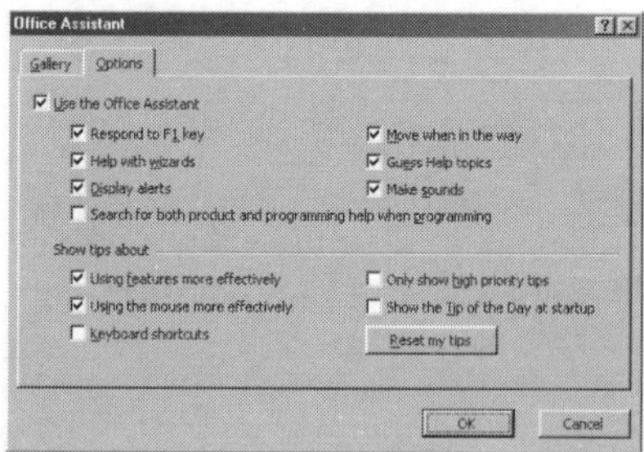

Figure 1.3 The Options tab in the Office Assistant dialog box allows you to set the options for this function.

The options you specify for the Office Assistant, as well as its look, will apply to all Office applications.

Help

If you have chosen to deactivate the Office Assistant, you must use the Help and/or Context Help icons to obtain Help.

Context Help

Context Help is a help option which matches the context in which you are working; you can also get help for a command, a button, and so on.

To obtain Context Help, click on the ? (question mark) in the Help Menu bar and select **What's This?** The pointer becomes a question mark. Click on the button or the command for which you require help. A ScreenTip is displayed, which describes the command or button (see Figure 1.4).

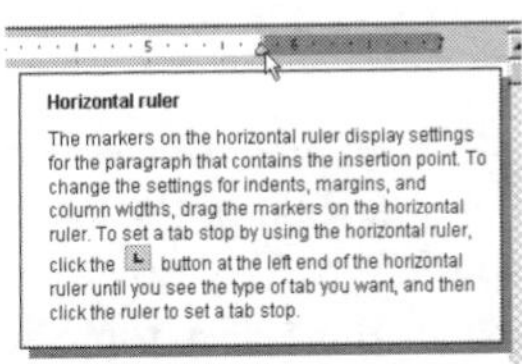

Figure 1.4 The ScreenTip describes the item you have just selected.

To obtain a Context Help in a dialog box, click on the ? (question mark) in the dialog box, then on the button or the command for which you require help.

Help icons

To open the Help summary, click on the ? (question mark) in the Menu bar, then select **Name of application Help.** A window opens on the right side of the screen. You need to know that:

- **The Contents tab** displays a list of topics. Double-click on a topic to display it.
  - A closed book next to a topic indicates that it contains a list of detailed icons. Double-click on it to open the list.

- An open book next to a topic indicates that it is selected. Double-click on it to close the topic.
- A question mark next to a section icon indicates that there is detailed text about this topic. To open it, double-click on the question mark or on the topic label.

- **The Index tab** allows you to search a topic based on the command name. In the **Type keywords** box, type the text corresponding to the command you require. Box 3 displays a list of icons concerning the entered text. To display the topic which corresponds to your search, click on it in box 3: the topic is displayed on the right side of the window.
- **The Answer Wizard tab** allows you to refine your search for Help. Type a word corresponding to the topic you are looking for in the **What would you like to do?** box. The outcome of the search is displayed in the **Select topic to display** area. Double-click on the topic of your choice in the second box.

*To print a Help topic, display it, then click on **Print** in the toolbar.*

■ Wizards and templates

Office 2000 puts at your disposal a number of Wizards and templates that you can use to speed up the execution of your operations, and this is true for all its applications.

Templates

A template (with the .dot extension) is a default document into which you simply insert your text.

To select a template, click on **File, New** (see Figure 1.5). The various tabs in the **New** dialog box offer several templates.

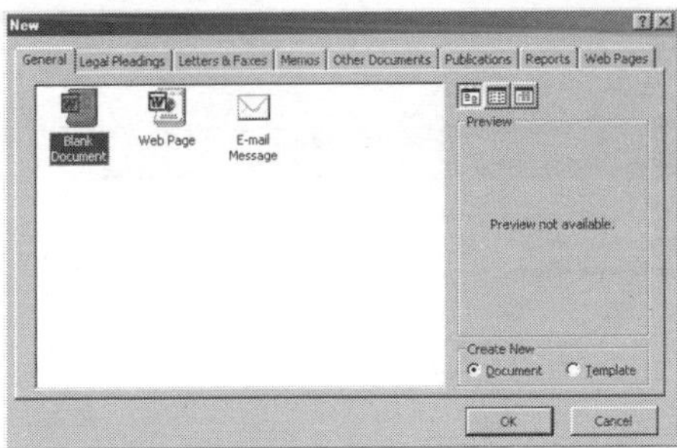

Figure 1.5 The tabs in the New dialog allow you to select a template.

Click on the tab which corresponds to your requirements, then double-click on the template you wish to use.

You can also access the choice of templates by clicking on the ***New Office document*** *button in the Office Manager Shortcut bar.*

To work with a template (see Figure 1.6), most of the time you simply need to modify the various text boxes. For example, in the **Click here and type name** text box, click on it, then type the required name. Before printing the template, just follow all the instructions. Obviously, the boxes with the instructions will not be printed.

Wizards

A Wizard is a sequence of dialog boxes where you specify your choice corresponding to the processing of a personal document.

To select a Wizard, click on **File, New.** The various tabs in the New dialog box offer several Wizards. Click on the tab which corresponds to your requirements, then double-click on the Wizard you wish to use. After completing the first stage, click on the **Next** button to move to the second,

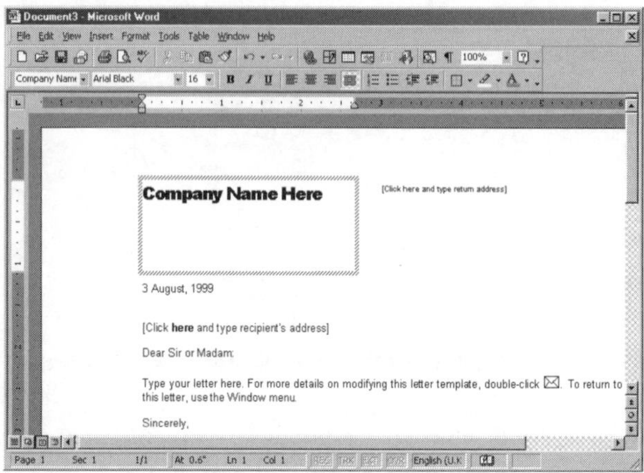

Figure 1.6 The Letter template.

and so on. Follow the various procedures, but if you have made a mistake or you wish to modify one of your choices, don't panic: click on the **Back** button to go back through the previous steps and modify your choice. Once you have finished the procedures, click on the **Finish** button and the document will be displayed on the screen. You can, obviously, implement customised formats by following the procedures included in the first chapters for each program.

*When, in a Wizard, you have clicked on the **Finish** button, you will not be able to go back.*

Creating a template

Although the number of templates available is fairly extensive, you still may not find exactly what you are looking for. The solution? Create them!

To create a template:

1. In the application, click on **File**, **New**. In the **Create New** area (underneath the Preview area), click on the **Template** option and then on **OK**.
2. Create the document template, specify the margins you require, the styles, and so on. When you have finished, click on **File**, **Save As**. You can also click on the **Save** icon in the Standard toolbar.
3. In the dialog box which is displayed, type the name of your template in the **Name** box, then click on **Save** (see Figure 1.7).

The application adds the created template to the existing ones. Whenever you wish to use it, therefore, you simply need to select it in the **New** dialog box.

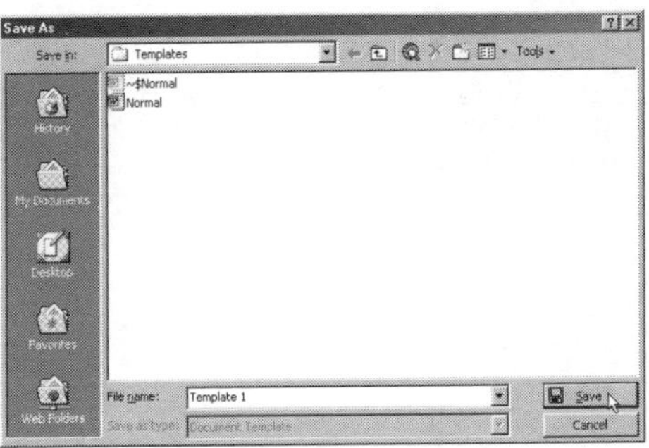

Figure 1.7 Enter the name of the template you want to create.

*When you save a template in the **Save As** dialog box, check that the **File type** box displays the document template. If this is not the case, click on the **Up One Level** button (the icon of a folder with an upwards pointing arrow), then select it.*

Spelling and Grammar check

Office 2000 allows you to check automatically spelling and grammar for documents, presentations, worksheets, and so on.

Automatic spellchecking

You can ask the application in which you are working to flag possible spelling errors. Click on **Tools, Options**, then click on the **Spelling and Grammar** tab and click on the **Check spelling as you type** option (see Figure 1.8). Click on **OK** to confirm.

Once this option has been activated, everything the software thinks is an error will be underlined with a wavy red line (see Figure 1.9).

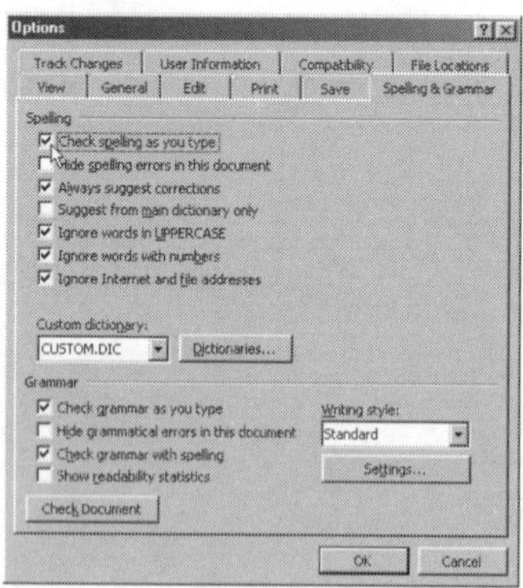

Figure 1.8 Activate Check spelling as you type.

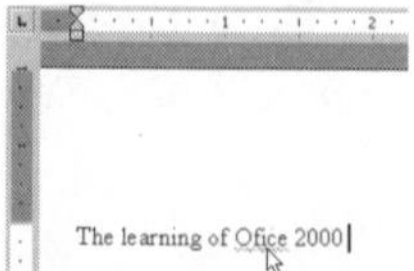

Figure 1.9 Spelling mistakes are underlined with a wavy red line.

To correct spelling errors, click with the right mouse button (right-click) on the underlined word, then select an option in the context menu.

- To select a word for correction, click on it.
- To add this word to the Office dictionary, click on **Add**.
- To ignore the error and to make sure that it is no longer shown as an error in the document, click on **Ignore All**.
- To choose another language (see the Activating another language topic), select **Language, Set Language**.

*If you have chosen not to activate automatic spelling and grammar checking, you can still check your documents with the **Spelling and Grammar** option in the **Tools** menu. Any word with spelling errors will be highlighted for you to correct it.*

Automatic grammar check

You can ask the application in which you are working to flag possible grammatical errors. Click on **Tools, Options,** then click on the **Spelling and Grammar** tab and click on the **Check grammar as you type** option. Click on **OK** to confirm.

Once this option has been activated, everything the software thinks is an error will be underlined with a wavy green line.

To correct grammar errors, follow the same procedure as for spelling.

Activating a language

In Office 2000, French, English, German, Italian and Spanish are recognised by default by the spellchecker, if installed. Therefore, when you need to correct a text written, for example, in French, not all the words will be underlined as errors, which is what used to happen. Only actual errors will be identified and the correction context menu will suggest the correct spelling. The available languages are marked with an ABC icon next to them in the list.

You can activate other languages. In any of the Office applications, click on **Tools**, **Language**, **Set language** (see Figure 1.10). Select the language you wish to add from the list and click on **OK**.

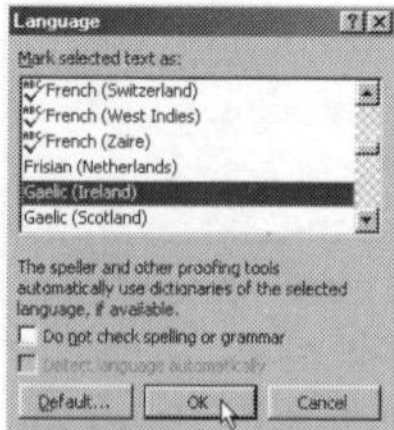

Figure 1.10 Activate other languages.

AutoCorrect

When you start working in an application, for example Word, you will notice that, when you enter a text, some misspelt words are immediately corrected. For example, if you have typed the word 'accomodate', this is automatically replaced with 'accommodate'. Furthermore, if you forget to start a sentence with an upper-case letter, the software replaces your lower case with an upper case. This is the AutoCorrect function. A list of words has been created in all the applications which tells the application how these should be spelt.

*If this option is not active, click on **Tools**, **AutoCorrect**. In the AutoCorrect tab, tick/clear the required options, then click on **OK**.*

The list of misspelt words with their correct correspondent word is not static: you can add your corrections to it.

To widen the scope of the AutoCorrect function:

1. Click on **Tools, AutoCorrect** (see Figure 1.11).
2. Type the misspelt word in the **Replace** box. Press the **Tab** key to move to the **With** box, then type the correct word. Click on **Add** to confirm this creation.
3. Click on **OK** to close the dialog box. You can create as many automatic corrections as you want.

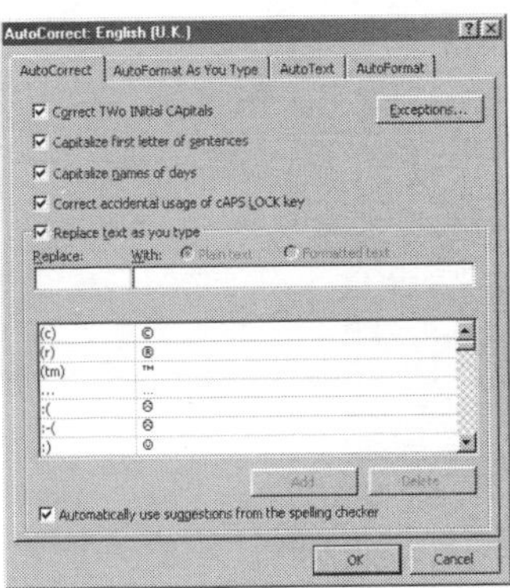

Figure 1.11 The AutoCorrect dialog box allows you to specify your correction parameters.

To delete an automatic correction, open the AutoCorrect dialog box. Select the word to be deleted in the list, then click on the **Delete** button. Then click on **OK**.

*The **Exceptions** button in the AutoCorrect dialog box allows you to specify exceptions for some corrections.*

Find and Replace

It may happen to any of us that we misspell a word throughout the document. This is not very difficult to correct manually if the document is only a few lines, but if the document is several pages long, Office suggests a better solution: the **Find** and **Replace** functions. The first allows you to search the whole document for the required word, the second replaces the required word with a different one.

To find and replace a word or a group of words:

1. Go to the beginning of the document by pressing the **Ctrl+Home** keys.
2. Click on **Edit**, **Find**, then click on the **Replace** tab (see Figure 1.12).

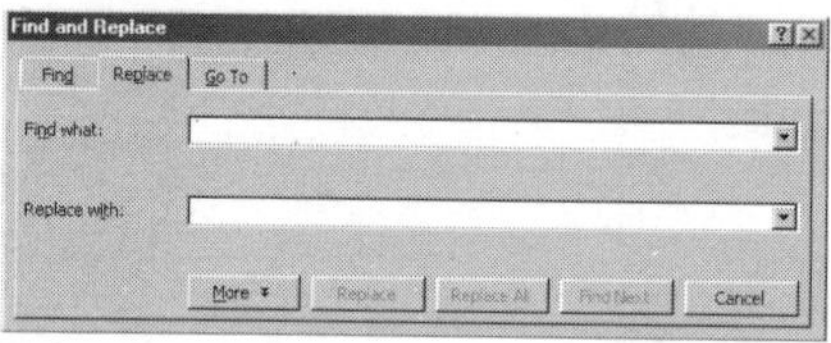

Figure 1.12 You can replace text quickly and easily with Find and Replace.

3. Type the word or group of words you wish to replace in the **Find** text box. Type the word or group of words to replace them with in the **Replace with** text box. You can refine your replacement by clicking on the **More** button. To start the search, click on the **Find Next** button.

   The first instance of the word you are looking for is displayed highlighted.
4. Click on one of the proposed buttons remembering that:
   a. **Find Next** goes to the next instance and ignores the selected one.
   b. **Replace** replaces the selected instance of the find criteria, finds the next occurrence and then stops.

c. **Replace All** replaces all instances of the find criteria in your document.

d. **Cancel** closes the dialog box without saving any changes you have made.

e. **Close** closes the dialog box and retains the changes you have made.

Finding synonyms

When you proofread your document, you may well find that the same word has been used too frequently. It would be better to find a synonym.

To find a synonym for a word, select the word, then click on **Tools, Language.** In the pop-down menu, select **Thesaurus** (see Figure 1.13). You can also press the **Shift+F7** keys. In the **Replace with Synonym** box there will be a list of words or expressions suggested as synonyms. In the **Meanings** box you can see the various dictionary meanings of the selected word. Choose a synonym and click on the **Replace** button.

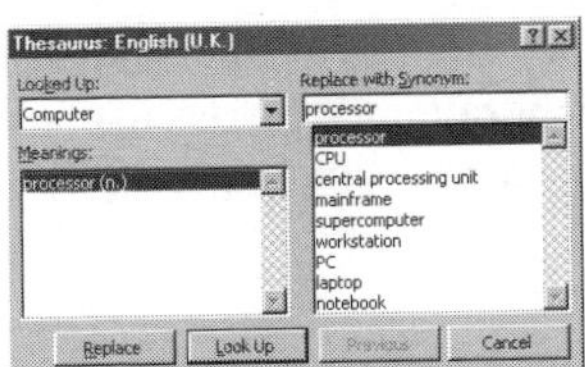

Figure 1.13 The Thesaurus allows you to search for synonyms.

■ Office 2000 and the Web

It is useless for us to launch into a long-winded explanation as to how to use the Web and how useful it is, as there are several other books dealing specifically with this subject. (*Internet* and *Internet Explorer 5* also from Prentice Hall).

Office 2000 comes with Internet Explorer 5, a Web browser. When you installed Office, this navigator was also installed. If you have a modem and an Internet connection, you can connect directly to the Web from Office.

Browsing the Web from Office

If you have a connection to a provider and are using Microsoft Internet Explorer as your browser, you can open Web pages directly from the Office applications with the Web toolbar. To display this toolbar, right-click on one of the active toolbars, then click on **Web** (see Figure 1.14). Then use the various buttons to carry out any operation you wish to execute.

Figure 1.14 The Web toolbar.

To access a discussion group from one of the Office applications, click on **Tools, Online Collaboration, Web Discussions**. Select the news server of your choice and simply get online.

Opening documents in Internet Explorer

Now, the compatibility of Office functions with Internet Explorer 5 allows all data in the browser to be retrieved once a document has been translated to HTML format. So, the complexity of PivotTables will be no problem for the browser: it will retain the original qualities of the document!

See Page 28 to learn more about how to save a document to HTML format.

To open a document in Internet Explorer once it has been saved in HTML format, click on **File, Open**. Select a file, then click on **Open**.

Web Preview

Once a document or a presentation has been saved in HTML format, you can view it in a Web Preview, so that you can see exactly the aspect your document will have when it is published on the Web.

To display a Web Preview for a document or a presentation, click on **File, Web Page Preview.**

Online collaboration

To implement an online collaboration from one of the Office applications, simply connect to the Internet. Then, click on **Tools, Online Collaboration, Meet Now**. Select the server name in the relevant option box. Netmeeting is launched, you can start to chat.

E-mailing from an application

You can now send a document by e-mail, from any Office application. Use the **E-mail** button, accessible from the Standard toolbar in all the applications. Once this command is active, the editing window for the message is displayed (see Chapters 9 and 10). Get information on the various options, then send your message.

Creating hyperlinks

A Web page is not complete unless it has hyperlinks. A hyperlink allows you to direct the visitor, with a simple click, to another part of the page or to another page in the site. All Office 2000 applications have an icon which allows you to insert hyperlinks to other documents, files or pages.

 To change a standard text into a hyperlink quickly:

1. Select the text, then click on the **Insert Hyperlink** button in the Standard toolbar (see Figure 1.15).
2. You must specify the URL (e-mail address) of the page to which the link goes. Type the hyperlink name in the **Type the file or hyperlink name...** option, or select the address in the list, or else click on the **File** button, then select the one to which the hyperlink is directed. Click on **OK.**

Top marks for PowerPoint. Its 2000 version allows you to automatically create a résumé to the left of the site. Once you have displayed the presentation in the navigator, simply click on one of the points you wish to be included in the résumé to display its contents directly in the window on the right (see Chapters 7 and 8).

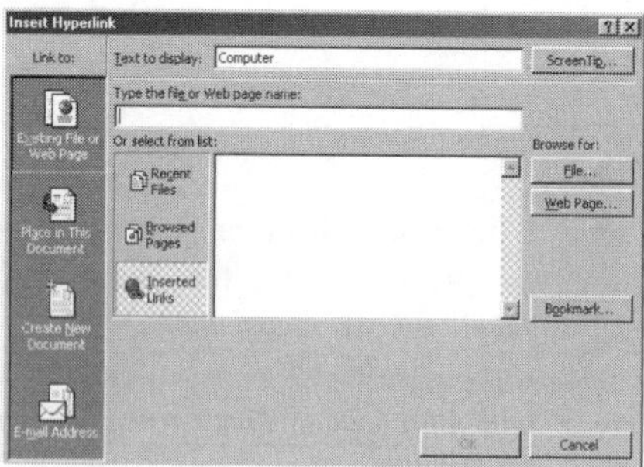

Figure 1.15 The Insert Hyperlink dialog box.

2 Shared commands

In this second chapter we will look at the functions and commands shared by all Office applications.

Undo/Redo an action

You can undo or redo an action that you have just executed. These functions are like an eraser in the Undo case, and like a paste-up in the Redo case: these allow you to undo or redo quickly the action or the command.

Clicking on this button undoes the last action. If you wish to undo several actions, click on the small arrow and select all that you wish to undo. You can also click on **Edit, Undo name of action.**

Click on this button to redo the last action you have just undone. If you wish to redo several actions, click on the small arrow and select all that you wish to redo. You can also click on **Edit, Redo name of action.**

*If you wish to repeat your last action, press the **F4** key.*

Start/Quit an application

When you have installed Office, the names of the various applications are placed in the **Start** menu, in **Programs**.

How to launch an application

To launch an application, click on **Start, Programs, Application name** (see Figure 2.1). You can also open an application by clicking on the corresponding button in the Office Manager.

The other solution is to place shortcut icons on your Windows desktop. This function is useful for common

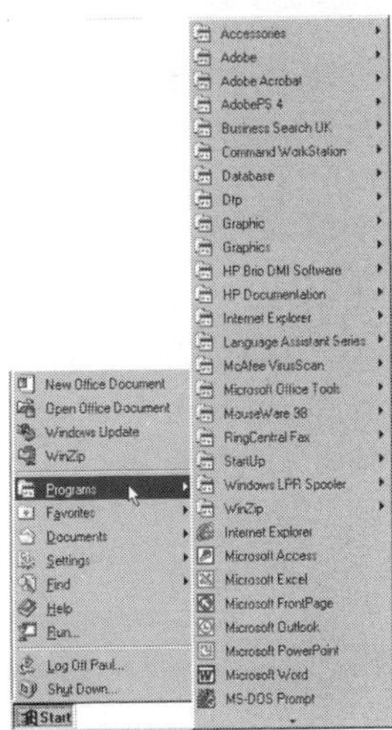

Figure 2.1 Start the application of your choice with Start, Programs.

applications, because you will simply need to double-click on this icon to launch the program quickly.

To create a program shortcut icon, click on **Start, Programs.** Click with the right mouse button on the program of your choice, then keeping the button pressed, drag it onto the Desktop. In the context menu which is displayed, select **Create Shortcut.**

Quitting an application

To close a program, several solutions are offered:

- Click on **File, Close.** If a file is open, you will be asked if you wish to save it or not. Click on Yes or No.
- Click on the **system** box, top left of the screen, which displays the program icon, then click on the **X** (Close).
- Press the **Alt+F4** keys.

Interface elements

All the elements in this section are shared by all the applications running under Windows 95 and 98. It is not our intention here to show you the procedures for using your system, but we believe that you should be acquainted with some basic principles.

Menu bar

The Menu bar is positioned underneath the Title bar. Each menu (File, View, and so on) opens a pop-down list which offers several commands (see Figure 2.2). Menus follow a number of parameters:

- Greyed commands are not available, commands in black are available.
- An arrowhead next to a command indicates that the command has a submenu.
- Three suspension points after a command indicate that the command opens a dialog box which allows you to select some options, specify some choices, and so on.
- A button positioned in front of a command indicates that the command can also be found as a shortcut in one of the Toolbars.
- A keys combination, such as a **Ctrl** or **Alt** followed by a letter, displayed next to a command confirms that this command also has a keyboard shortcut. By pressing these keys, you will automatically open the command or its dialog box (for example, with the **Ctrl+P** keys, you open the Print dialog box).

To make your tasks easier, the 2000 version allows automatic menu customisation. Therefore, while you are working,

File Edit View Insert Format Tools Table Window Help

Figure 2.2 The Menu bar in Word.

menus get adapted to your choice and display only what you are using. To view a complete menu, simply click on the two arrowheads, or chevrons, at the bottom of the menu, or double-click on the menu name (for example, double-click on File to view the default menu).

Dialog boxes

In addition to the **Open** and **Save** dialog boxes there is the **Position** bar which looks the same as the Outlook one. This allows quick access to the most used folders and documents. Also, dialog boxes have been made larger for better viewing. Finally, some dialog boxes include a button which allows you to return quickly to recently used folders or files. This button is easily recognised: it is an arrow pointing to the left.

*The **Back** button is the same as the one used in the Internet browsers.*

Toolbars

Positioned underneath the Menu bar, toolbars allow quick access to some of the most commonly used commands. By default, programs display two toolbars: **Standard** and **Format.** However, you can display several others.

To display a toolbar, click with the right mouse button on a toolbar and select the required toolbar from the menu.

To hide a toolbar, right-click on a toolbar and click on the one you wish to hide.

Previously static and not really very attractive, toolbars are now '*à la carte*': they take up little space because they are displayed one next to the other and because they change according to the user's needs. To view the whole of a toolbar, simply click on the two arrowheads which point to the right, on its right edge.

The toolbar customisation options are now simplicity itself.

To customise a toolbar once you have it on the screen:

1. Click with the right mouse button on **any toolbar** and, at the bottom of the drop-down toolbar menu, select **Customize.**
2. In the Customize dialog box, the **Options** tab allows you to specify exactly the display (large icons, list of fonts, ScreenTips, and so on). The **Toolbars** tab allows a toolbar to be activated and new ones to be created, while the **Commands** tab lists the various categories of buttons as well as their icons.
3. To add an icon to a toolbar, select the category, click on the button to be added in the list on the right and drag it into the relevant toolbar. Click on **Close** to confirm.

To delete a button, click on the arrowheads in the relevant toolbar, select **Add/Remove buttons** (see Figure 2.3), then click on the option check box against the command to be removed.

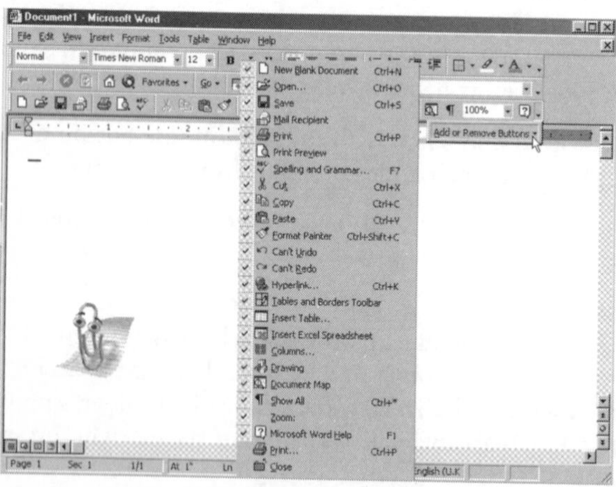

Figure 2.3 You can easily turn off a toolbar button.

Saving data

To save a document, a worksheet or even a slide, simply click on the **Save** button in the application Standard toolbar or click on **File, Save.** The procedure is very different depending on whether you are saving the file for the first or the nth time.

To save the first time:

1. Click on the **Save As** command in the File menu (see Figure 2.4).
2. Select the folder in the **Save in** area or use the Views bar by clicking on the folder (for example **My documents**).
3. Type the name of the file to be saved in the **File name** box (do not type the extension, this is automatically generated by the application from which you are saving). Click on the **Save** button.

When you save the document the next time, simply click on the **Save** button in the Standard toolbar.

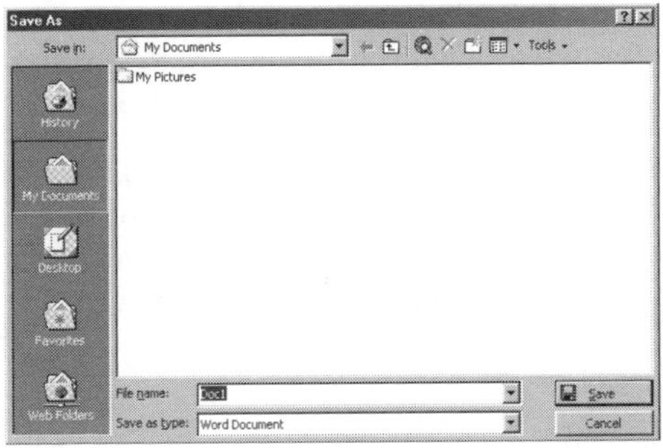

Figure 2.4 The Save As dialog box.

Save documents to HTML format

The HTML format is the format used on the Web. Whatever the document you wish to publish (text, presentation, worksheet, and so on), you must change it to an HTML document before publishing it. Without this transformation, it will not be readable on the Web.

To save a document or a presentation to HTML format:

1. Click on **File**, **Save as Web Page**.
2. Name the file in the **Name** box. You can edit its title by clicking on the **Change Title** button. Click on **OK** in the **Set Page Title** box (see Figure 2.5), then on **Save**.

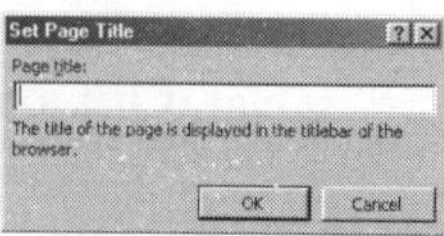

Figure 2.5 Changing the name of your Web page.

Save on a server

  You can now save a document directly onto a server, for example on your company's Intranet.

To save a document on a Web server, click on **File**, **Save as Web Page**. In the Views bar, click on **Web Folders**, which contain possible shortcuts to the Web server(s). Select the server of your choice. Name the document and click on **Save**.

■ File management

The concept of file will be familiar to you if you have some experience in using the computer. On the other hand, if you are a beginner, here are some explanations. In Windows, when you create a document, a table, a presentation, and so on, you create a file. Files are 'kept' in folders. You can see all the files in your computer in Explorer.

Opening files

To open a file, you must click on the **Open** button in the Standard toolbar or on **File, Open** (see Figure 2.6). Select the folder which contains the required file in the **Look in** box or using the Views bar. Then, simply double-click on the file.

*To open a recently opened file, click on **File**: the file is displayed at the bottom of the menu. Then simply click on it to open it. If the program is not open, you can also click on **Start**, **Documents**. The list of the last fifteen used files is displayed. Select the one you wish to open.*

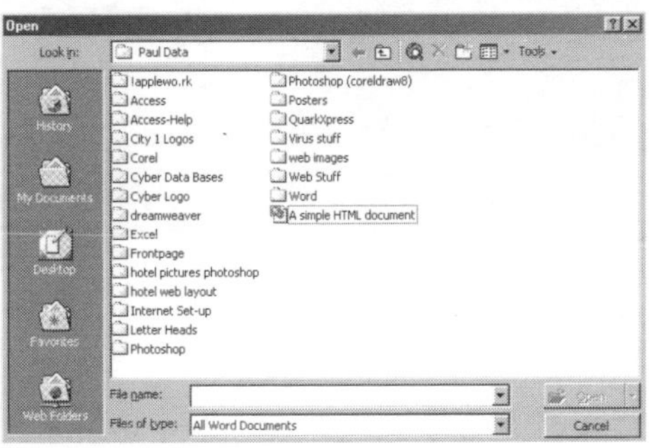

Figure 2.6 Opening a file in the Open dialog box.

Closing files

To close a file, either click on the **Close** window button (shown by an **X**), or click on **File, Close**.

Deleting and renaming files

To delete a file, click on the **Open** button. In the dialog box, click with the right mouse button on the relevant file and select **Delete**. Click on **Yes** to confirm the deletion.

To rename a file, click on the **Open** button. In the dialog box, click with the right mouse button on the relevant file and select **Rename**. Type the new name and press **Enter** to confirm.

■ Printing

First switch on your printer, then click on the **Print** button. If you wish to specify the printer to be used, the number of copies to be made, and so on, you must click on **File**, **Print**, then specify your choice in the Print dialog box (see Figure 2.7). Click on **OK** to confirm your choice and start printing.

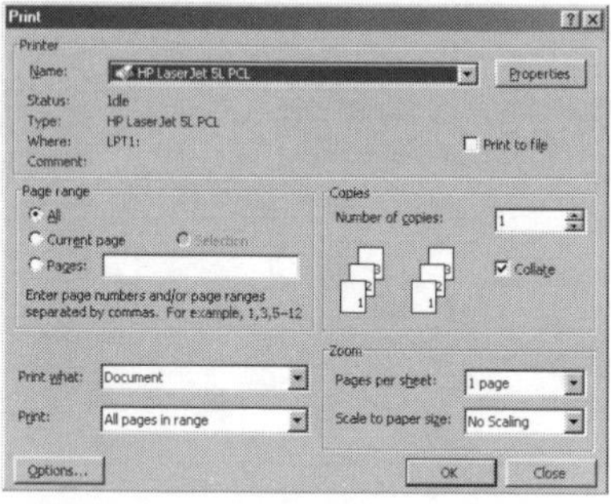

Figure 2.7 The Print dialog box in Word.

■ Cut, copy, paste and move

When creating documents, you may need to move, cut or copy a word, a sentence, an object, and so on. These procedures are extremely simple.

To copy, select the element you want, then press the **Ctrl+C** keys. You can also click on **Edit**, **Copy**.

To cut, select the relevant element, then press the **Ctrl+X** keys. You can also click on **Edit**, **Cut**.

To paste an item, press the **Ctrl+V** keys. You can also click on **Edit, Paste.**

To move, select the item on your document, then click on the selection. Keeping the mouse button pressed, drag to where you wish to move it to. Release the mouse button.

You can also use the **Copy**, **Cut** or **Paste** buttons. Their procedures are identical to those we have just seen.

■ Clipboard as-u-like

When, in a document, you copy or cut part of a text, an object, and so on, with the **Edit, Copy** or **Edit, Cut** commands, the element is stored in the **Clipboard**, which is a sort of waiting room. Then you can paste the contents of this Clipboard into another document or another page.

In previous versions of Office, when you copied or cut an item, the action deleted automatically the previous Clipboard contents. This is no longer the case. Now, you can store up to twelve items in the Clipboard. When you wish to paste an element, simply select it in the Clipboard.

When you cut and/or copy several items, the Clipboard toolbar is displayed automatically (see Figure 2.8). Position your cursor where you wish to insert one of these items. Click on the item of your choice in the Clipboard toolbar: the item will be inserted in the document.

*If the Clipboard toolbar is not displayed, click with the right mouse button on a toolbar and select **Clipboard**.*

Figure 2.8 The Clipboard toolbar.

■ Inserting text styles

With WordArt, you can create texts which stretch, become curved, create angles or even display characters in 3D.

To insert a WordArt text object:

1. Click on where you wish to place it, then on **Insert, Picture, WordArt** (see Figure 2.9).
2. Click on the style, then confirm by clicking on OK.
3. A new dialog box is displayed; enter the text to which the selected style will be applied. Make various formatting choices such as font, size, attributes, and so on, then click on **OK**.

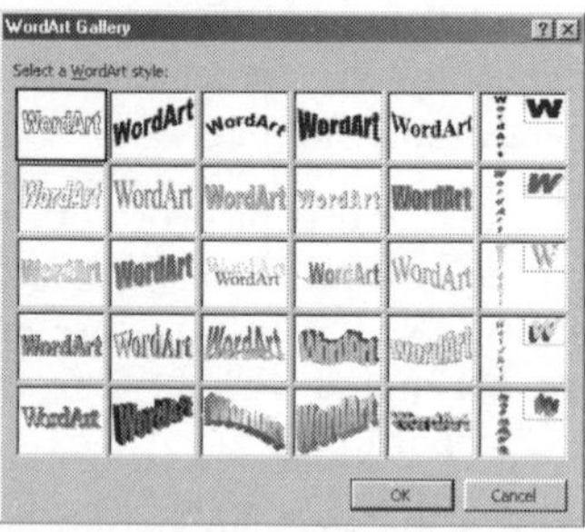

Figure 2.9 The WordArt subapplication allows you to create titles, subtitles and so on.

The text is inserted in the document (see Figure 2.10).

Text Styles

Figure 2.10 Place WordArt text to add the finishing touches to a document.

Moving, resizing, copying and deleting a WordArt object

A text created with WordArt corresponds to a graphic object: when you select it, it becomes surrounded by small squares known as *handles*, which allow the object to be moved, resized, and so on.

To move a WordArt object, click on it, then, keeping the button pressed, drag it to where you wish to go and release the button.

To cut, copy and paste a WordArt object, use the Copy, Paste and Cut commands in the Edit menu or use the corresponding buttons.

To resize the WordArt object, click on one of its handles and drag it in the required direction.

To delete a WordArt object, click on it to select it, then press the **Del** key.

WordArt toolbar

The WordArt toolbar which is displayed when you select the text object allows you to modify and to format this object. Table 2.1 shows the various buttons it contains as well as their functions.

Table 2.1 WordArt toolbar buttons

Button	Action
	Inserts a new WordArt object into the page.
Edit Text...	Modifies the text of the WordArt object.
	Selects another style for the WordArt object.

Button	Action
	Modifies size, position and colour for the object, and places the text around it.
	Selects another shape for the WordArt object.
	Displays the round handles around the object to make it rotate.
	Defines text wrapping.
	Puts all the object characters at the same height.
	Displays characters vertically.
	Modifies text alignment.
	Modifies character spacing in the WordArt object.

Copying a format

Office does things very well: not only is formatting characters quick and easy, but it is also possible to copy the various formatting choices in two stages, with three actions.

To reproduce a format, select the word or the sentence, click on the **Format Painter** button on the Standard toolbar. The pointer becomes a paintbrush. Drag it on to the word or the sentence in which you wish to copy the format. Release the button. To copy the formatting to more than one item, double-click and then click on each item you want to format. When you are finished, press **Esc** or click again to turn off the **Format Painter**.

Inserting pictures

Office allows insertion of pictures into any document. Pictures are all proposed in the ClipArt Office 2000 gallery, which also contains sound files and animated clips.

Inserting a personal picture

When you insert pictures into a document, you will make it easier to understand, clearer and, above all, more original. You can insert a picture that you have scanned or found on the Web.

To insert a picture that you have saved:

1. Click on **Insert, Picture, From File.**
2. Select the type of graphic file you wish to insert. Select the folder which contains the file. For the picture to be inserted into your page, double-click on the file which contains it.

Inserting a ClipArt picture

ClipArt offers a vast number of pictures that you can insert into a document as you wish.

To insert a ClipArt picture:

1. Click on **Insert, Picture, ClipArt** (see Figure 2.11).
2. All pictures are accessible from the **Pictures** tab. They are classified by category. To view the contents of a category, simply click on it. Once you have made your choice, click on the picture to be inserted, then, keeping the button pressed, drag it into the document and release the button.

If you need to insert several pictures into your document, you can leave ClipArt open to be able to return to it quickly. To display it again, click on the button in the Taskbar.

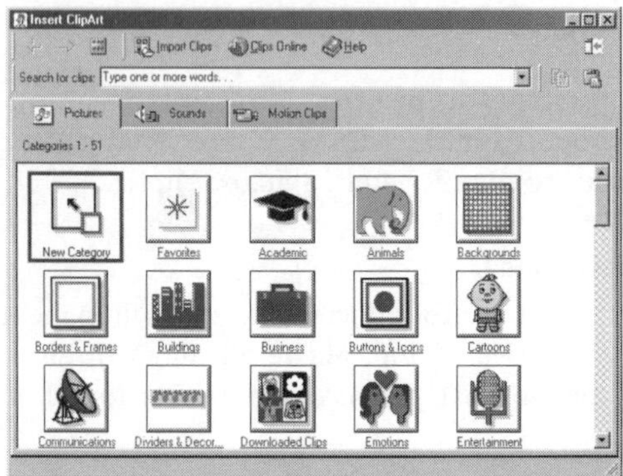

Figure 2.11 Choose an image from the ClipArt library.

If you do not have much time and you want to find a picture quickly, open the ClipArt dialog box, type the term which describes the picture in the **Search for clips** box, then press the **Enter** key.

Refer to Chapters 7 and 8 for further information on how to edit a picture.

The Web is a gold mine for those who need pictures. In fact, there are thousands of sites where you can retrieve pictures to use in a document.

Pictures downloaded from a site but which are not in the public domain cannot be used for commercial purposes.

To find a picture on the Web:

1. Open ClipArt. Click on the **Clips Online** button in the toolbar. Obviously, you must be connected to the Internet.
2. In the dialog box which is displayed, click on **OK**: the navigator is launched. Surf the Web. In the site which contains the picture you like, select the picture: this is automatically inserted into ClipArt.

3 Basic Word functions

New document

Entering text

Moving within the text

Selecting

Correcting text

Views

Formatting text and paragraphs

Formatting pages

In this third chapter, you will learn Word basic functions such as entering text, formatting it, modifying the view, and so on.

New document

By default, when you launch Word, a blank document and the Office Assistant are displayed.

To open a blank document, click on the **New** button. You can also click on **File, New**. If required, click on the **General** tab (see Figure 3.1), then double-click on **Blank Document**.

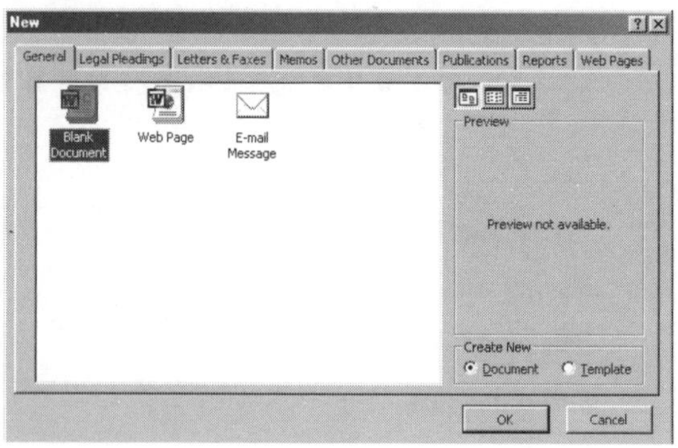

Figure 3.1 Open a new document.

The Word screen

Before going any further, let us examine the screen and its various items (see Figure 3.2). From the Menu bar you can access all the Word functionalities; the various toolbars offer shortcut buttons for the more often used commands or functions. The flashing cursor is the default insertion point for your text. Scroll the vertical or horizontal scroll bar to move within the page.

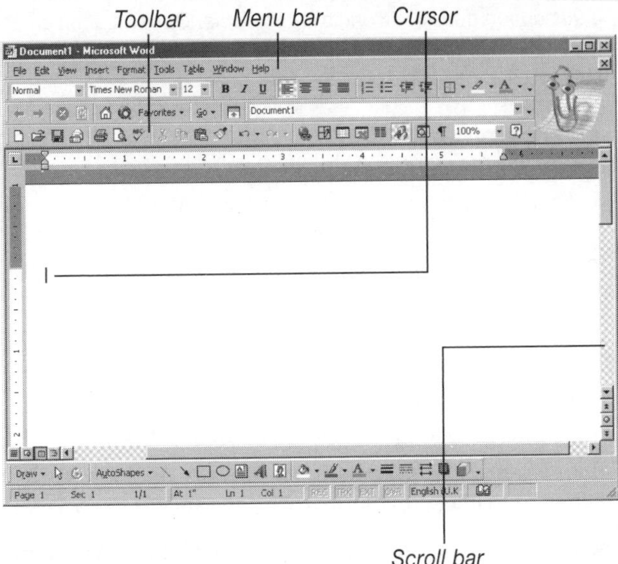

Figure 3.2 The Word screen.

■ Entering text

These are some of the rules and tips you need to know when entering text:

- By default, the flashing cursor, or insertion point, shows the position for the text you are going to enter.
- Have you noticed? Now, when you move the cursor on the page, it displays some small dashes on its right. If you wish to enter text somewhere other than at the beginning of the page, simply double-click on where you want to be, then start typing: Word will look after formatting by itself. It is truly click and type.

If this option does not work, click on ***Tools, Options****, then on the* ***Edit*** *tab. Tick the* ***Enable click and type*** *option, then click on* ***OK****.*

- Typing is very fast: Word does automatic line feeds when you reach the right margin.
- To create a new paragraph, press the **Enter** key. This procedure also allows insertion of a blank line.
- To go to a new line without creating a new paragraph, press the **Shift+Enter** keys.
- At the bottom of the page, the horizontal line marks where the page ends. If you wish to insert text beyond this line, Word automatically creates another page. To insert a forced page break, press the **Ctrl+Enter** button.
- Avoid using tab keys to create indents in the text. It is better to manage this format with the **Indent** keys.

When you create paragraphs or insert blank lines, Word generates characters known as *non-printing characters*. To view them, click on the button which displays the **Show/Hide formatting marks** symbol in the Standard toolbar. You can also click on **Tools, Options.** In the View tab, click on the icon in the **Formatting marks area**, then click on **OK** to confirm your choice.

Non-breaking hyphens, non-breaking spaces and accented upper case

When typing, Word automatically executes carriage returns. When words must not be split, and to avoid Word inserting the first part of a compound word on a line and the second on another, you must create a non-breaking space or a non-breaking hyphen.

To create a non-breaking space, type the first word, then press the keys **Ctrl+Shift+Spacebar**. Type the second word and again press **Ctrl+Shift+Spacebar**.

To create a non-breaking hyphen, type the first word, press **Ctrl+(8) lower case**, then type the second word.

When you type titles or any other text in upper case, Word does not display accents. For more sophisticated entry, you can create titles with accented upper-case characters.

To insert accented upper-case characters:

1. Click on **Insert, Symbols** (see Figure 3.3).
2. Click on the accented upper-case character you wish to insert. Click on the **Insert** button, then on the **Close** button.

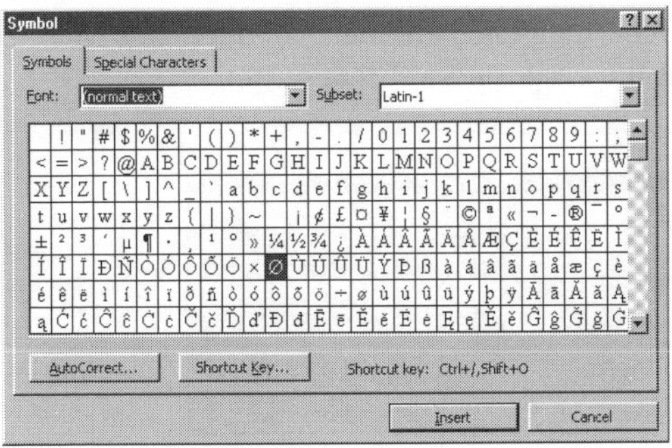

Figure 3.3 Use Symbols for accented capital letters.

■ Moving within the text

These are the procedures you need to follow to move within a text:

- Point to where you want to be, then click.
- Scroll the vertical or horizontal scroll bar in the direction of your choice (up, down, left or right). A little box will appear: this shows the number of the page which will be displayed if you release the mouse.

- Click on the **Previous Find/Go To** or the **Next Find/Go To** arrows to display the previous or the following page. These arrows are positioned at the bottom of the vertical scroll bar.
- Click on one of the arrows at the bottom of the vertical scroll bar to scroll the text up or down. Release the mouse button when the text is displayed.

Going to a specific page

To go to a specific page, click on **Edit, Go To** (see Figure 3.4). Type the page number, then click on the **Next** button. To go to a specific item in your document, in the Go to what list, click on the item, then enter the item number, and click on the **Go To** button. Click on the **Close** button.

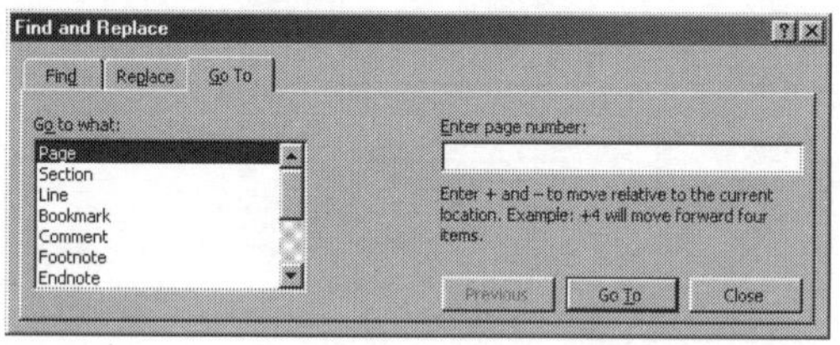

Figure 3.4 Use the Go To tab to display a page or specific element.

Selecting

For all text manipulations (moving, copying, deleting, formatting, and so on), you must already have selected your text. Selecting consists of marking the text on which you want to act. A text selected will be shown as highlighted (in reverse).

To select a word, click on the beginning of the word, then drag the mouse over it keeping the button pressed.

To select a group of words, click in front of the first word to be selected, press the **Shift** key, then, keeping the mouse button pressed, use the direction keys.

To undo a selection, click outside the selected item.

■ Correcting text

Once your text has been entered, you may want to insert something, replace or even delete one or several words:

- To insert a word or a character into an existing text, click where you want to insert something, then type the new word or the new character.
- To replace a word with another one, double-click on the word, then type the replacement word.
- To delete text, select it, then press the **Del** key.
- To clear text positioned before the insertion point, press the **BkSp** key.
- To clear text positioned after the insertion point, press the **Del** key.

■ Views

When you launch Word, a new document is displayed: it corresponds to a page, but you can see only half of it. You are in Page view, which is the default display view. When creating a document, it is occasionally necessary to modify the display of pages. Word includes several possibilities for different display of pages on the screen: these are the Display and Zoom views.

Display views

Each proposed display view allows execution of a specific task. You can access these various views by opening the View menu, then selecting the display view to be activated. You can also use the display views buttons positioned in the bottom left corner of the document.

The display views buttons proposed are the following:

- **Normal View.** Displays pages as a long text divided into pages by automatic page breaks. This mode is easy to use, because it requires very little memory.
- **Web Layout View.** Shows the document as it would look in a Web navigator when published on the Web.
- **Print Layout View.** Displays the document as it will appear when printed. This view, which takes up much memory, slows down the scrolling of the document.
- **Outline View.** This allows you to display the structure of your document, giving you the chance to modify it (see Figure 3.5).

Zoom

The option Zoom allows you to modify exactly the size of the page on the screen.

To modify the size of the zoom, click on the arrow in the **Zoom** pop-down list, then select the display percentage. You can also double-click on the text box, then enter the percentage and press the **Enter** key to confirm.

Switching between several documents

It is possible to work simultaneously on several different documents.

To switch between various documents, click on **Window**. At the bottom of the menu, the list of open documents is displayed. Click on the document you wish to display.

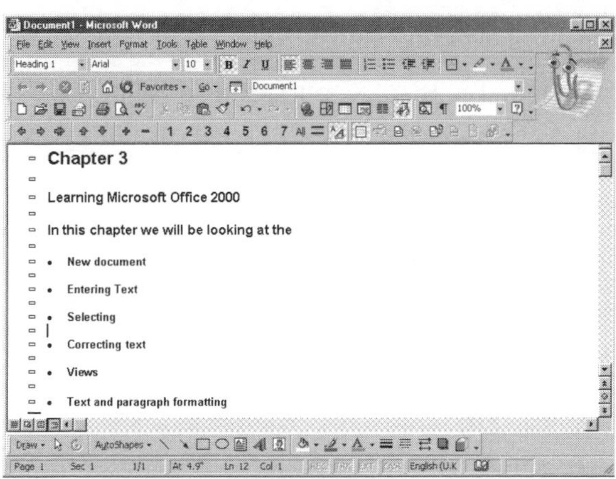

Figure 3.5 A document in Outline View.

To display several documents on the screen, click on **Window**, then select **Arrange All** (see Figure 3.6).

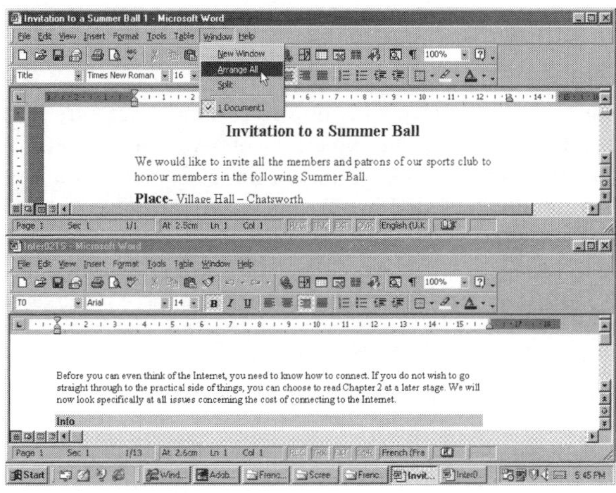

Figure 3.6 You can display several documents on screen.

Formatting text and paragraphs

Word default font is Times New Roman, 10 points, without attributes; paragraphs are left-aligned, have a space before and after 0 and have no indent.

*A paragraph is a set of characters which finishes with a carriage return executed with the **Enter** key.*

Formatting procedures

You can define the format for characters and paragraphs before or after entry:

- **Format before entry.** Select the various formats as explained in this chapter, then type the text.
- **Format after entry.** Select the text, then choose the various formats required.

To format a single word, there is no need to select it: simply click on it, then choose the various formatting options.

Quick character formatting

The simplest and quickest method to format characters is to use the Format toolbar. In Table 3.1 you will find the various formats proposed. Some of the buttons displayed on this toolbar are not included in this table: refer to Quick paragraph formatting to learn about their use.

Table 3.1 Buttons proposed for formatting characters in the Format toolbar

Button	Action
Times New Roman ▾	Modifies font.
10 ▾	Modifies text size.

Button	Action
B	Executes bold.
I	Executes italic.
U	Underlines text.
	Selects underline colour.
A	Selects colour.

To delete a format, select the relevant text, then click on the attribute to deactivate it.

Sophisticated character formatting

The Font dialog box allows you to select all the character format options.

To use the Font dialog box (see Figure 3.7), click with the right mouse button on the selection text to be formatted and choose **Font.** Carry out your format choice, then click on **OK.**

This is what can be done in the other tabs in the Font dialog box:

- **Character Spacing.** Allows you to modify spaces between characters as well as text kerning.
- **Text Effects.** Allows you to animate the text. This function is important only if you are transferring your document as a file and not on hard copy.

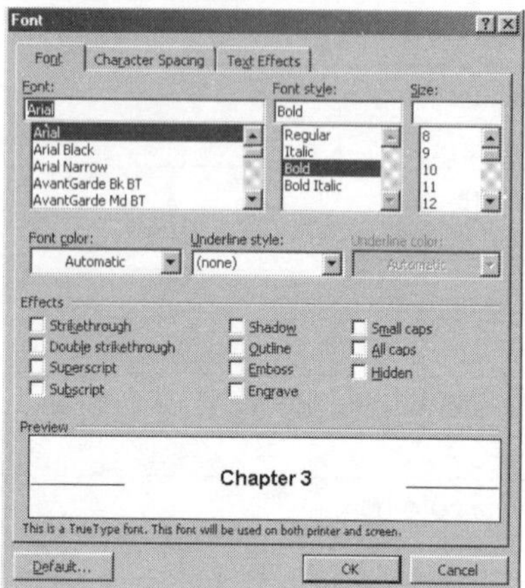

Figure 3.7 The Font dialog box allows you to select all the options for character formatting.

To modify the character case (upper case, lower case), click on **Format, Change Case** (see Figure 3.8). Select the option, then click on **OK**.

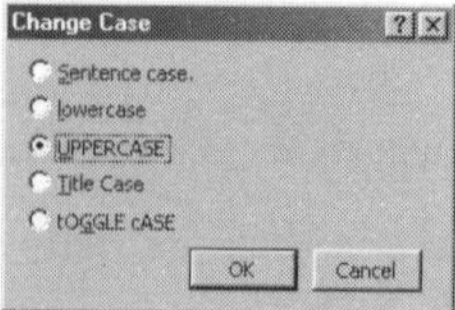

Figure 3.8 The Change Case dialog box offers several case options.

*The **tOGGLE cASE** option allows you to display in upper case a text which was in lower case, and vice versa.*

Quick paragraph formatting

The simplest and quickest method to format paragraphs is to use the Format toolbar. In Table 3.2 you will find the various formats proposed.

Table 3.2 Buttons for formatting paragraphs in the Format toolbar

Button	Action
	Flush aligns the paragraph to the left margin.
	Centres the paragraph between left and right margins.
	Flush aligns the paragraph to the right margin.
	Spreads the text in the paragraph over the whole width of the page, between left and right margins.
	Creates a numbered list.
	Creates a bulleted list.
	Decreases the value of the paragraph indent in relation to the left margin.
	Increases the value of the paragraph indent in relation to the left margin.
	Frames a paragraph.

To delete a paragraph format, select the paragraph, then click on the relevant button to deactivate it in the Format toolbar.

Sophisticated paragraph formatting

The Paragraph dialog box allows you to select all the paragraph format options.

To use the Paragraph dialog box (see Figure 3.9), click with the right mouse button on the text selected for formatting and choose **Paragraph.** Execute your formatting choices, then click on **OK.**

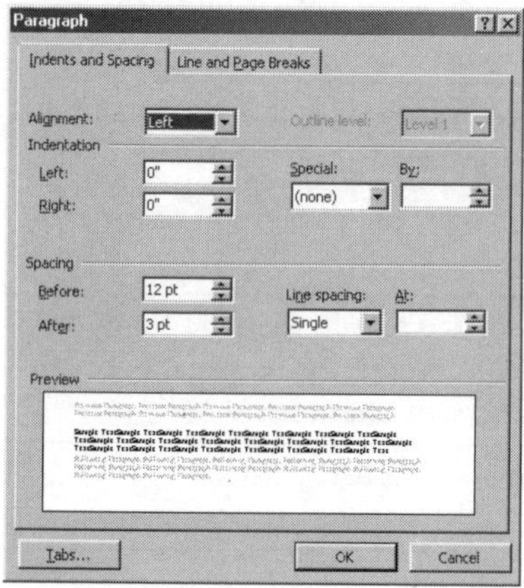

Figure 3.9 The Paragraph dialog box allows you to select paragraph formatting options.

This is what the Paragraph dialog box allows you to do:

- **Indents and Spacing.** Allows you to modify paragraph alignment, indents and spacing. Alignment allows you to define the position of paragraphs in relation to the margins (see Figure 3.10). Indents apply either to the whole of the paragraph, or to its first line (see Figure 3.11); they allow you to indent the text in relation to the left margin. You can also modify indents with the ruler (see Figure 3.12).

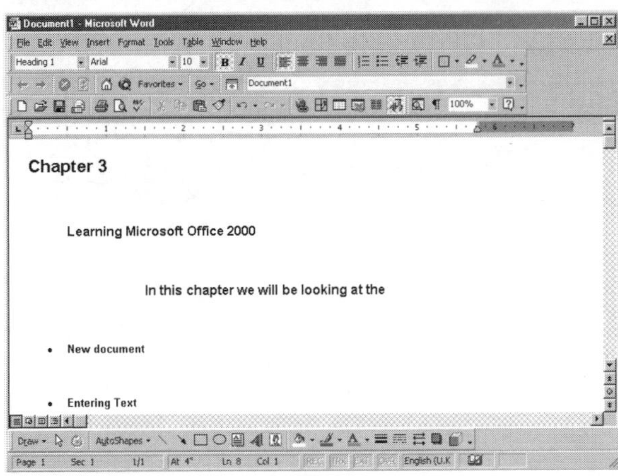

Figure 3.10 The various ways of aligning text.

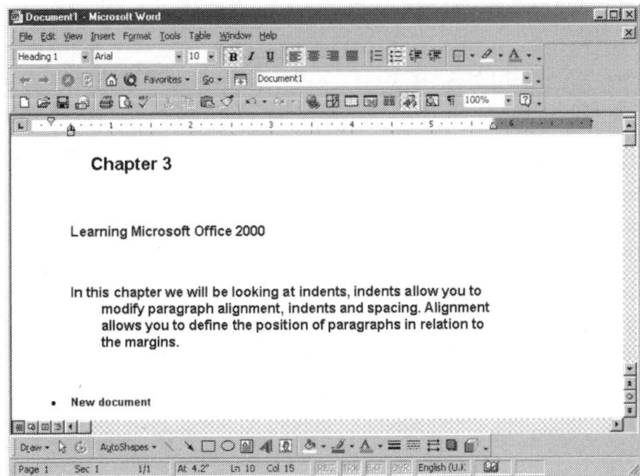

Figure 3.11 Examples of indents.

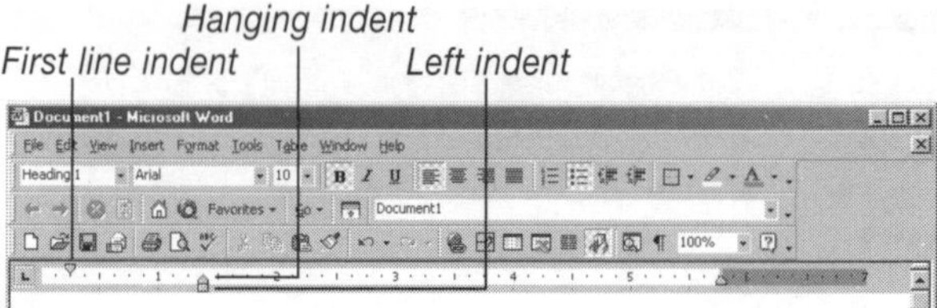

Figure 3.12 Using indents on the ruler.

- **Line and Page Breaks.** Allows you to define the position of the paragraph in relation to the other paragraphs. For example, you can request the paragraph not to be split at the end of the page.

*To undo paragraph formats and go back to the default options, select the relevant paragraph, then press the **Ctrl+Q** keys.*

Bulleted lists

Bulleted lists allow you to add or remove bullets from a selected text.

To create a bulleted list quickly, use the **Numbering** or **Bullets** buttons proposed in the Formatting toolbar (see Table 3.2). When you click on one of these buttons, Word inserts a number or a bullet (a graphic element). Each time you enter an item in the list, simply click on the **Enter** key and the next number or a new bullet will appear. When you have finished entering the bullet list, press the **BkSp** key or click on the relevant button in the Formatting toolbar to deactivate it.

You can modify the bullet or the type of number displayed in the bullet list.

To modify bullets or type of number:

1. Click with the right mouse button on the bullet list and select **Bullets and Numbering** (see Figure 3.13).

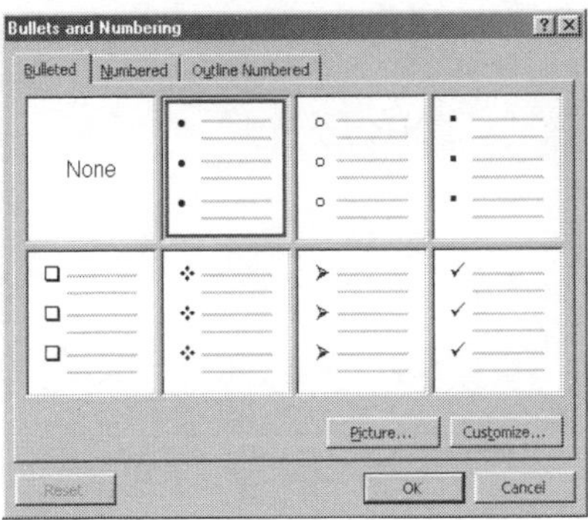

Figure 3.13 The Bullets and Numbering dialog allows you to modify the numbering or bulleting of your lists.

2. Click on the tab corresponding to your choice (**Bulleted** or **Numbered**). Click on the type of bullet or number you want. The **Customize** button allows you to select other types of bullets. Click **OK** to confirm your choice.

Borders and shading

The Borders and Shading functions allow you to frame a paragraph and to display it in grey.

To create the border and the shading for a paragraph:

1. After having selected the paragraph, click on **Format, Borders and Shading.** Click on the **Borders** tab (see Figure 3.14).
2. Select the style for the border, then choose the settings. You can modify the colour and the width of the border. If you wish to colour the background of the paragraph, click on the **Shading** tab. Choose the fill colour, the shading pattern, then click on OK.

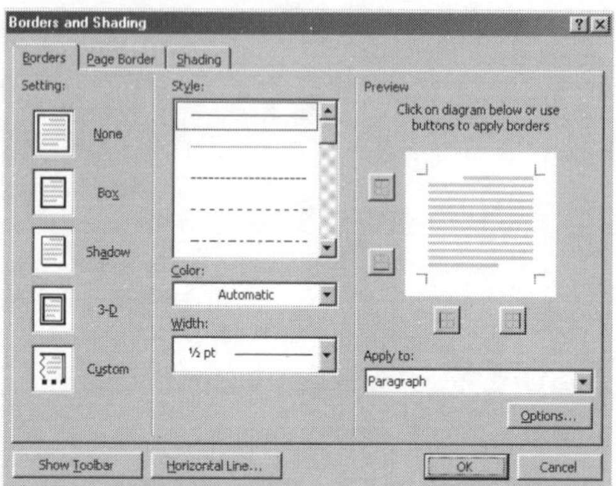

Figure 3.14 The Borders tab of the Borders and Shading dialog.

*To delete a border, click on **Format**, **Borders and Shading**. Click on the **Borders** tab, then select **None** in the border style. Click on **OK** to confirm your choice.*

■ Formatting pages

Word includes commands to enhance your page: you can therefore frame the whole of a page, assign a coloured background or a picture background, and so on.

Framing a page

To frame your page, you must use the Borders and Shading function (see previous page).

Background

You can assign a background to your page or to the whole document. You need to know that the background chosen will not print and that it will be seen only in the Web view.

This function is therefore useful when you publish your document on your company's Intranet or on the Web or even if you send it to someone on diskette.

To choose a background, click on **Format, Background.** In the pop-down menu which opens, click on the colour corresponding to the one you want. You need to know that the **More colours** option opens a dialog box with two tabs: the **Standard** tab allows you to select another colour, the **Custom** tab allows you to define exactly the required colour by specifying the percentage for each component colour. If a simple background colour is not enough, click on the **Fill effects** option. In the Fill effects dialog box and its various tabs, you can choose a gradient, a texture (droplets, mosaic, and so on) and a pattern. Click on **OK** to confirm your choices.

You can also opt for a picture as a background. This will appear as a watermark on the whole page. You have two possibilities: either using a picture from one of your files, or a ClipArt picture (see Chapter 2).

To choose a background picture:

1. Open the **Fill effects** dialog box as explained above. Click on the **Picture** tab, then the **Select Picture** button.
2. Select the file which contains the picture you wish to display as background. Click on **OK**.

*To delete a background, either in colour, as a pattern or as a picture, click on **Format, Background**. In the pop-down menu, click on **No fill**.*

Inserting a header and a footer

To insert a header or a footer, click on **View, Header and Footer.** A specific toolbar is displayed. The header will be shown framed by dots. Simply enter your wording, then use the various Header and Footer buttons in the toolbar.

Formatting

This is the last stage before sending your document to print. You will learn how to define margins for your document, its orientation and its pagination.

To execute formatting:

1. Click on **File, Page Setup** (see Figure 3.15). You need to know that:

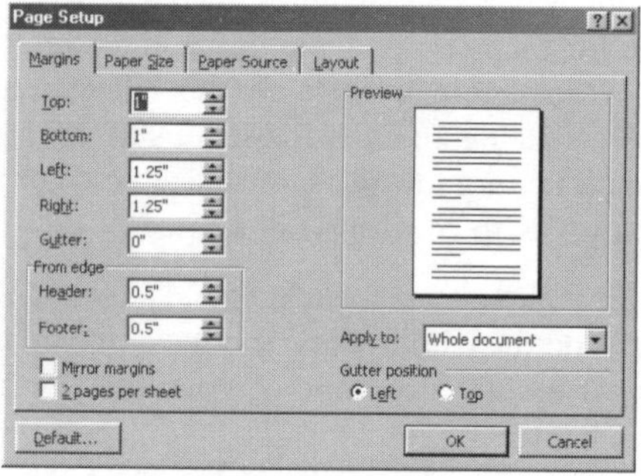

Figure 3.15 The Page Setup dialog

   a. **Margins tab** allows you to modify the margins for your document and to define gutters, if you need to. The **Mirror margins** option is for recto-verso printing. The **Preview** area displays the defined choice. The **Apply to** option, by clicking on its arrow, opens a pop-down list in which you select the part of the document to which formatting applies.
   b. **Paper Size tab** allows you to choose the orientation of your document (Portrait, vertical, or Landscape, horizontal).
   c. **Paper Source tab** allows you to define the printer feed for this print job.

d. **Layout tab** allows you to define the position of the text in your document (vertical or horizontal alignment). You can also choose to number lines in your document.

2. Click on the required tabs, then execute your choices.
3. Click on **OK** to confirm them.

4 Advanced Word functions

Creating a table

Creating columns

Mailshots

Automatic format with styles

We have now reached the stage where we are able to look at more sophisticated functionalities in Word, such as creating tables, using mail merge, and so on.

Creating a table

Each time you have difficulties in aligning two text blocks or any other element, you can use the Table function. A table is made up of rows and columns. Their intersection creates cells.

To draw a table

The Draw Table option allows you to create the general outline for your table. Once this is done, you split it into several parts by tracing lines and columns.

To draw a table:

1. Click on **Table, Draw Table**. The pointer becomes a pencil.
2. Click on the page where you wish to insert the table. Drag to draw a rectangle which will form the frame for your table (see Figure 4.1). Draw rows and columns to complete the table.

To customise rows and columns, you can select their format in the ***Tables and Borders*** *toolbar before drawing them.*

3. Once you have finished the 'drawing', click on **Table, Draw Table** so that the pointer goes back to its original shape.

Use the eraser to clear incorrect rows or columns. This button is available in the Tables and Borders toolbar.

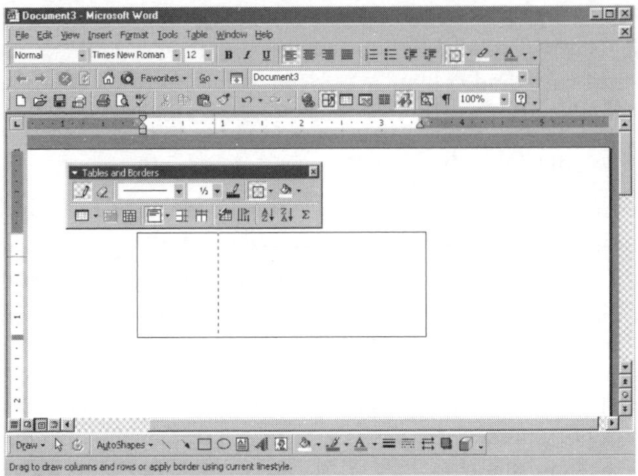

Figure 4.1 The Draw Table function allows you to create the outline for your table.

Inserting a table

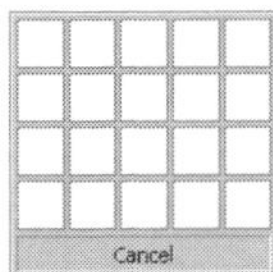

To create a table quickly, simply click on this button: a little frame is displayed, which shows rows and columns for a table (see Figure 4.2). Simply drag the mouse over it to select the number of rows and columns you require for the table. The textual description of the number of rows and columns selected is displayed at the bottom of this frame. Once you have finished, release the mouse: Word inserts the table you have specified into the page.

Figure 4.2 With the Insert Table button you can quickly create a table.

Table dialog box

The Table dialog box allows you to specify exactly the number of rows and columns. You can assign up to 63 columns to a table.

To use the Table dialog box:

1. After having clicked where you wish to insert the table, click on **Table, Insert Table** (see Figure 4.3).
2. Type the number of columns in the **Number of columns** box. Type the number of rows in the **Number of rows** box. In the **AutoFit behavior** area, select your choices. The **Auto** choice inserts columns of equal size between the document margins. The **AutoFormat** button automatically applies predefined formats to your table, including borders and shading.
3. Click on **OK** to confirm your choices.

The table defined in the Insert Table dialog box will be shown in your document.

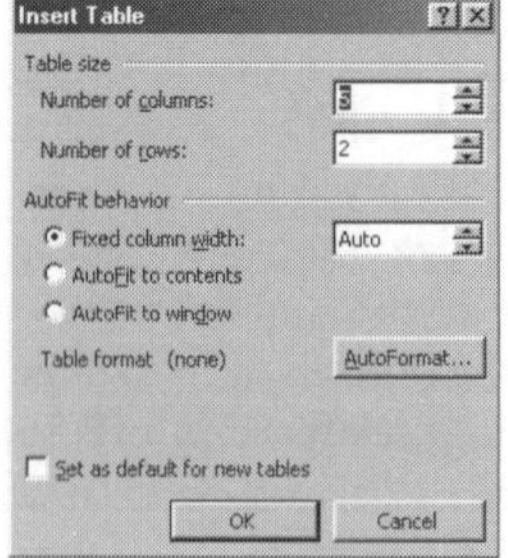

Figure 4.3 You can specify the number of columns and rows in your table in the Insert Table dialog.

Moving within a table

Before starting to enter data in the table, you must be able to move quickly within it. Refer to Table 4.1 to see how you can achieve this.

Table 4.1 Moving within a table

To	Press ...
Go to the next cell	Tab
Go to the previous cell	Shift+Tab
Go to the first cell in the line	Alt+Home
Go to the first cell in the column	Alt+PageUp
Go to the last cell in the line	Alt+End
Go to the last cell in the column	Alt+PageDown

Selecting within a table

Once your table has been created, you will be able to format it, add rows, columns, assign a border, and so on. But to execute all this formatting, you must know how to select the various items. Table 4.2 indicates the selection procedures.

Table 4.2 The various selections in a table

To select	Procedure
A cell	Point to the intersection of column and row, then click.
A column	Point to the top border of the column, then click.
A row	Point to the left border of the row, then click.
The whole table	Table, Select, Table.
The text of a following or previous cell	Tab or Shift+Tab.

Inserting, deleting cells and rows

Once the table has been produced, you must know how to edit it by deleting cells, adding rows, and so on.

Now, you can draw a table within a table. Insert a table with the procedure shown above, then click on a cell and repeat the procedure – **Table, Insert Table** (see Figure 4.4).

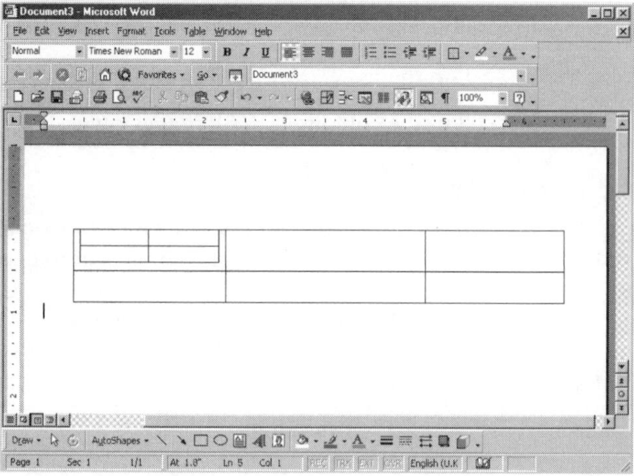

Figure 4.4 You can insert a table into a table.

To insert a cell, select a cell, then click on **Table, Insert Cells** (see Figure 4.5). Click on the option, then on OK.

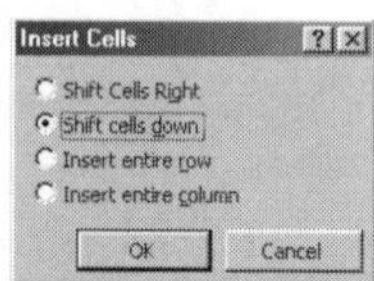

Figure 4.5 You can insert a cell into a table.

*To delete a cell, select it and press the **Del** key.*

To insert a row, click on **Insert**, then select the option. There is a faster method: click on the row below where you wish to insert the new row, then click on the **Insert Rows** button in the Tables and Borders toolbar (the little arrow next to the Insert Table icon).

*When you wish to insert four rows, for example, select them in the table, then click on the **Insert Rows** button. Word automatically inserts four empty rows into the table.*

To insert a column, select the column before the insertion, click on the **Insert Columns** button in the Tables and Borders toolbar. You can also click on **Table, Insert Columns.**

*To delete a row or a column, select it, and press the **Del** key.*

Orientation and display of the title row

You can change the orientation of text in cells. Click on the relevant cell, then on the **Change Text direction** button in the Tables and Borders toolbar.

When you create a table with several rows, not all the table will be visible on the screen. It is then difficult to enter text in the table: pretty soon, you start to get mixed up because you can't see the column header. The best solution is to leave the title for all columns permanently displayed at the top of the page by selecting the title row then by clicking on **Table, Titles.**

Formatting tables

To format a table – and not the characters in the various cells – you can choose one of these methods:

- **AutoFormat.** After having selected the table, click on **Table, Table AutoFormat.** Select the template, then click on OK.
- **Borders and Shading.** After having selected the table, click on **Format, Borders and Shading** (see Figure 4.6). Click on the **Borders** tab, then choose the border in the **Style** area. Specify the type in the relevant area. Click on the **Shading** tab if you wish to assign a shading to the table. Define your choices, then click on **OK.**

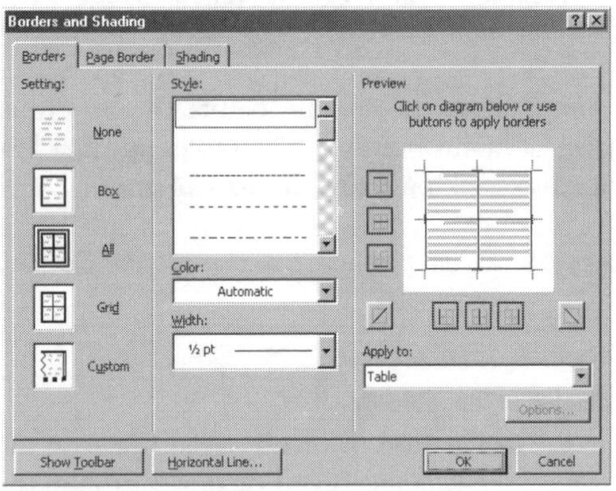

Figure 4.6 The Borders and Shading dialog.

■ Creating columns

There are two methods of creating columns. The first consists of clicking on the **Columns** button in the Standard toolbar, then selecting the number of columns you wish to apply. The second consists of clicking on **Format, Columns** (see Figure 4.7), selecting the appropriate **Presets** option and clicking on OK.

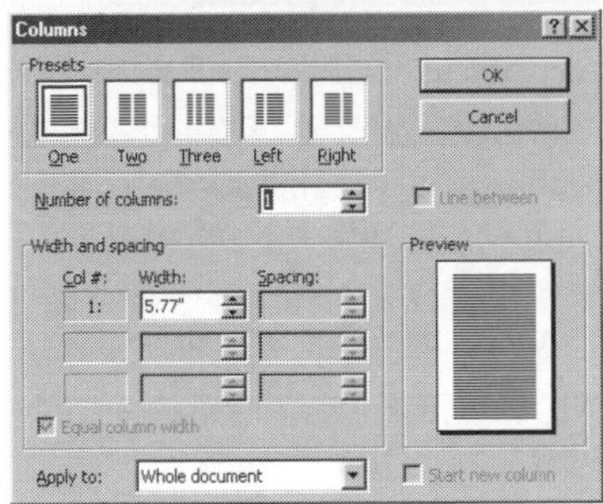

Figure 4.7 Choose the number of columns in the Columns dialog.

Once you have created columns, simply insert your text with the following procedures:

- Just type away: Word automatically 'wraps' to the next line when you reach the end of the column.
- To go to the following column, click on **Insert, Break,** then select the type of break in the Break dialog box. The page break goes to the next page, the section break goes to the next column.

*Have you inserted a column break and columns are no longer balanced? To balance columns, insert a **Continuous break**.*

■ Mailshots

When you need to send several people an identical letter, use the Mail Merge function and its various elements:

- **Main document.** The basic document to which your variable data will be added when doing a mail merge. These are placed in the relevant fields according to various criteria.

This document contains only the text which is common to all the letters you need to print as well as the fields where the various variables are going to go when merging occurs.

- **Data source.** The document which contains all the variable data. The variable data is inserted into the relevant fields when merging occurs. It is in fact the database to which the main document refers when printing the letters.
- **Merge fields.** Areas in your main document where the data from the data source will go.
- **Merge.** A command which allows you to create letters and merges the main letter with the contents of the variable data source. Once this merge is executed, you can print your letters directly or display them on screen.

Main document

The first thing to do is to create the main mail merge document, which is the letter you are going to send to all the people you are including in your mailshot.

To create the main document:

1. Click on the **New** button, then, when you have the blank document on screen, click on **Tools, Mail Merge** (see Figure 4.8).
2. Click on the **Create** button, then select **Form Letters**. A new dialog box is displayed, which asks if you wish to create your letter from your active document or if you wish to display a new document. If you have followed the procedure, click on **Active Window**. If this is not the case, click on **New main document** and type the text for your form letter as you usually would.

If you wish to create the main document from an existing document, open the relevant file and click on ***Tools, Mail Merge****. Click on the* ***Create*** *button in the dialog box Mail Merge Helper, select the* ***Form Letters*** *option, then click on the* ***Active Window*** *button.*

Figure 4.8 The Mail Merge Helper makes it easy for you to choose and merge all the different elements.

Data source

Once your main document has been created, you must enter the various data you wish to be inserted into it. This is the step when you actually create the database. Since you have just created the main document, the Mail Merge Helper dialog box is still displayed.

To create the database:

1. In the Mail Merge Helper dialog box, click on the **Get data** button in the second area (Data source). Click on **Create Data Source.** The **Use Address Book** option allows you to use, as a database, one of your address books (see the chapters on Outlook).

   The **Create Data Source** dialog box is displayed. Here you are going to select the fields you need to insert into the form letter (name, surname, address, town, and so on). The **Field names in header row** list is displayed with all the proposed fields (see Figure 4.9).

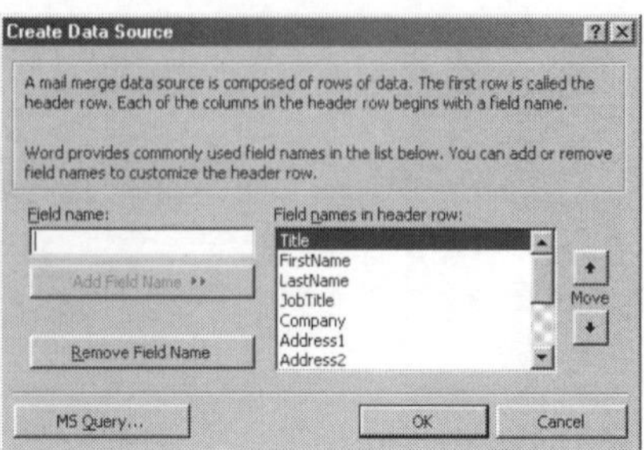

Figure 4.9 You can define the various field names in the Create Data Source dialog.

2. Format the set of fields in the following way:
   a. Delete the fields which are not relevant by clicking on them, then by clicking on the **Remove Field Name** button. The deleted field will disappear from the **Field names in header row** list.
   b. To add a field, enter it in the **Field name** option and click on the **Add Field Name** button. The defined field is displayed in the **Field names in header row** list.
   c. To move one of the fields in the **Field names in header row** list up or down, select the relevant field, then click on the arrow pointing to the direction you want (on the right of the list).
3. When you are satisfied with the fields and their position, click on **OK**.
4. Save the database as prompted by Word.
5. Click on **Edit Data Source** to start entering the various data to be used for the merge.

*If you have already created a database, open the Mail Merge Helper dialog box, click on the **Get data** button and select **Open Data Source**. Now simply select the database you wish to use.*

Entering data

When you have chosen the **Edit Data Source** command, a dialog box is displayed: Data Form. This is made up of the various fields you have already defined in Create Data Source. Type your merge data (the list of your mail merge addressees) and use the **Tab** key to move from field to field. When you have finished entering a record, click on **OK** to confirm and exit from the database or click on the **Add** button to display a new record to enter.

*To edit a data record, click on the **Edit Data Source** button in the Mail Merge toolbar. Now just carry out your modifications.*

Merging

Before starting the merge, you must instruct Word as to where you wish to insert data on the page.

To insert merge fields:

1. If necessary, right-click in a toolbar, then select **Mail Merge** to display it. Click where you wish to position the first merge field (usually surname or name).
2. Click on **Insert Merge Field** in the Mail Merge toolbar. Select the first field to insert into the list which opens (see Figure 4.10).
3. Repeat these procedures for all the fields you wish to insert.

   You must achieve the type of document which is shown in Figure 4.11.

Before starting the merge, you should check your work. Click on the **Check for Errors** button in the Mail Merge toolbar. In the **Checking and Reporting Errors** dialog box, click on your choice, then on OK. If everything is as it should be, Word displays a dialog box to confirm that no errors were found. Click on **OK**.

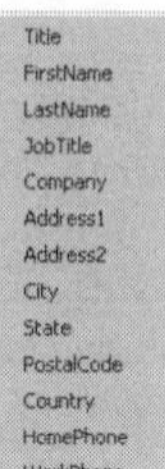

Figure 4.10 The Insert Merge Field drop-down menu.

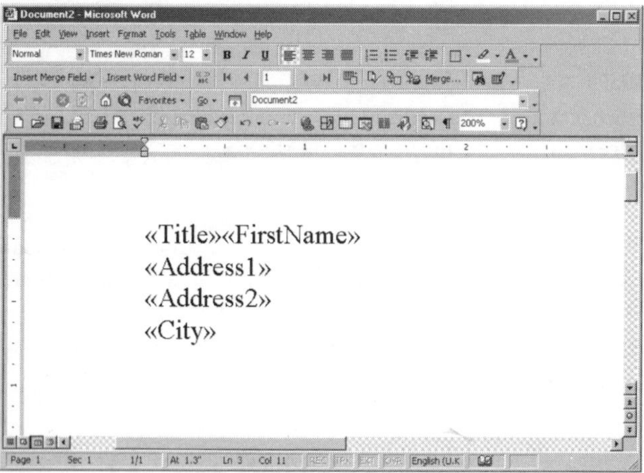

Figure 4.11 The main document with merged fields.

You are now ready to start the merge: click on the **Merge** button in the Mail Merge toolbar. Several options are proposed for the merge in the **Merge To** area:

- **Merge To.** Allows you to merge directly to a new document, to your e-mail program or even allows you to print letters.

- **Records to be merged.** Allows you to print the letters for the addressees selected in the data source only (see further down in this chapter).
- **When merging records.** Specifies to Word if it must or must not print blank lines when data fields are empty.
- **Query Options.** Displays a dialog box from which you can sort the merged letters or filter your data so that your letters are printed only for a specific type of addressee, selected among all the data.

Once you have defined your choices, click on the **Merge** button. If you have started the merge to the printer, Word prints the letters. If you have chosen to save the merge in a new file, the letters are displayed in a new document.

To create a query when merging occurs – that is, to apply a sort to the data and only print or create letters corresponding to this criterion (for example, you have decided only to create letters addressed to people living in London) – open the Mail Merge dialog box and click on the **Query Options** button. Type the query items, then click on **OK**. Then repeat the procedures shown above to start the merge.

Automatic format with styles

A style is a set of formatting characteristics (size, alignment, attributes, and so on) which can be applied to a paragraph or to a character. This function allows you not to have to repeat applying formatting options when the document contains several pages.

Choosing a style

Word 2000 offers a certain number of styles which you can apply to paragraphs or to characters.

To choose a style:

1. Click in the relevant paragraph or select the required words. Click on the little arrow in the **Style** button (see Figure 4.12).
2. Select the style.

   The paragraph is now displayed with the selected style attributes, and the Style button displays the active style in its text box.

Some styles apply only to paragraphs, others only to characters.

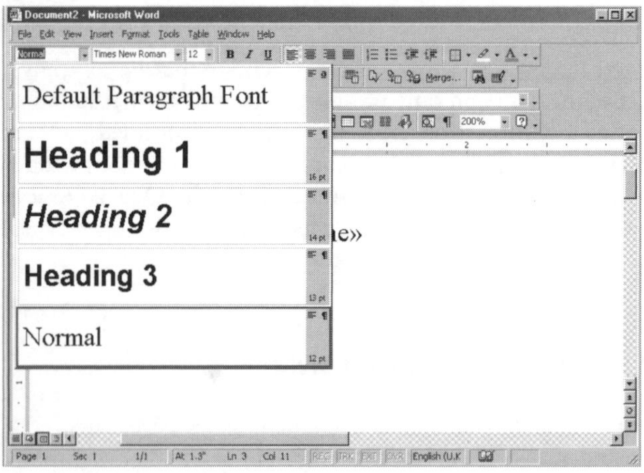

Figure 4.12 You can choose a style quickly with the Style button.

Creating a style

Even though Word offers a large variety of styles, it is quite possible that none of them is suitable for one of your documents. In this case, you can quickly create a personal style which you can then apply to all your documents.

To create a style, specify all the formatting (size, font, attributes, alignment, indent, and so on) and click on the arrow in the **Style** button. Type the name and press **Enter**. The style which you have just specified is now an integral part of the styles for this document. To apply it to another paragraph, simply click on the relevant paragraph, then select the style of your choice in the pop-down list from the **Style** button.

5 Basic Excel functions

The first step

Worksheet management

Data

Management of cells, rows and columns

Help with your entry

Format

We will now look at Excel basic functions such as how to enter data, how to manage a workbook and its worksheets, the functions which help with entering data and the various formatting procedures.

■ The first step

By default, when you launch Excel, a blank workbook is displayed. We have already seen how to open an existing workbook. To open a new workbook, simply click on the **New** button.

Screen

Before going any further, let us examine the screen and its various items (see Figure 5.1). From the Menu bar you can access all the functionalities of Excel; the various toolbars offer shortcut buttons to the most used commands or functions. The A1 cell (see below) is surrounded by a black frame which indicates that it is selected.

Microsoft has really caught up with the euro! When you launch Excel, a toolbar called EuroValue is displayed: this allows you to select functions which use the euro. If this is of no use to you, click on the **Close** button (symbolised by an X) in the Title bar.

Workbooks and worksheets

A workbook is made up of worksheets. By default, the workbook has three worksheets. Worksheets can be opened with the tabs positioned at the bottom of the workbook. Each worksheet is made up of little boxes known as 'cells'. These are arranged on a maximum of 256 columns, referenced from A to IV, and on 65,336 rows, referenced from 1 to 65,336. Each cell has the name of the intersection between the row and the column where it is placed. For example, the A5 cell is at the intersection of the first column and the fifth row.

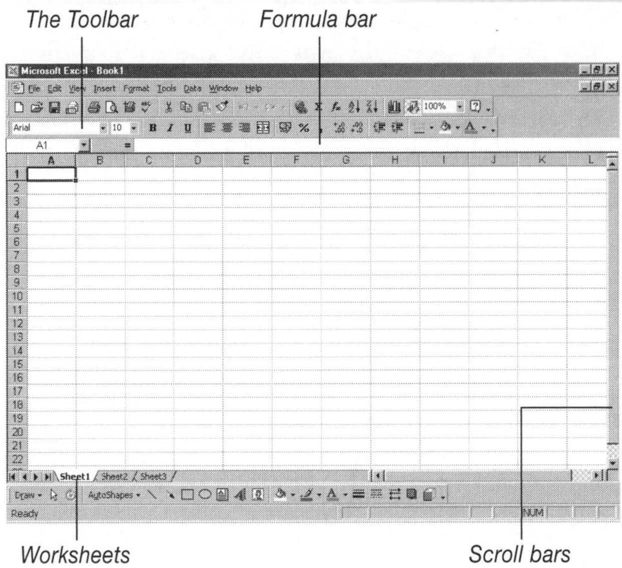

Figure 5.1 The Excel screen.

■ Worksheet management

As we have just seen, worksheets are the basic working tools. This being so, you must know how to move within them, how to add, delete, and so on.

Moving between worksheets

To move between worksheets or to select a specific one, you must use the tabs positioned at the bottom left of the screen. Here are some tips to speed up work:

- To move between worksheets, use the scroll buttons positioned to the left of the tabs. The two middle buttons allow you to go back or forward by one tab, the left button goes back to the first tab and the right button goes to the last one.

- Click with the right mouse button on one of the scroll buttons, then select the worksheet to be displayed (see Figure 5.2).
- To select several worksheets, press the **Ctrl** key, keep it pressed, then click on the tab of each worksheet to be selected.

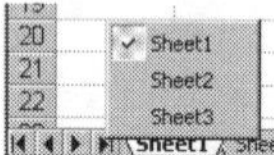

Figure 5.2 Choose which worksheet to view in the context menu.

Adding, deleting, copying and moving worksheets

By default, a workbook offers three worksheets. Let us now see how to add a worksheet, delete it, move it, and so on.

To add a worksheet, click on one of the tabs, then on **Insert, Sheet.**

To delete a worksheet, click with the right mouse button on its tab, then select **Delete.** Confirm its deletion (see Figure 5.3).

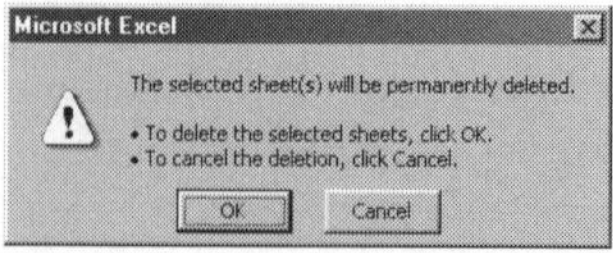

Figure 5.3 Confirm the deletion of the worksheet.

To move a worksheet within the workbook, click on its tab, then, keeping the button pressed, drag to the position of your choice.

To copy a worksheet in its workbook, click on its tab, then keep the **Ctrl** key pressed and drag to where you wish to place the copy.

To copy or move a worksheet to another workbook:

1. Open the two workbooks. Right-click on the tab of the worksheet you wish to move or copy. Select the **Move or Copy** option (see Figure 5.4).
2. Click on the arrow in the **To book** box. Select the workbook into which you wish to copy or move the selected worksheet.
3. In the **Before sheets** list, click on the worksheet in front of which you wish to position the new sheet tab. Click on **OK** to confirm your choice.

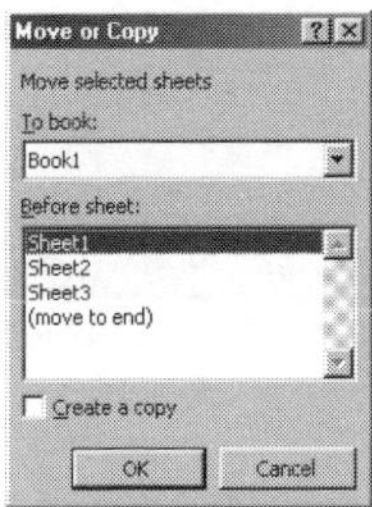

Figure 5.4 The Move or Copy dialog box allows you to specify into which workbook you want to copy your worksheet and its position in the book.

Hiding and showing a worksheet

You may wish to hide one of the sheets in a workbook. In fact, if your PC is connected to your company's Intranet, it may be better to hide some data.

To hide a worksheet, select it and click on **Format, Sheet**. Select **Hide**.

To view a hidden worksheet, click on **Format, Sheet.** Click on **Unhide.** In the dialog box (see Figure 5.5), click on the worksheet you wish to display and click on **OK.**

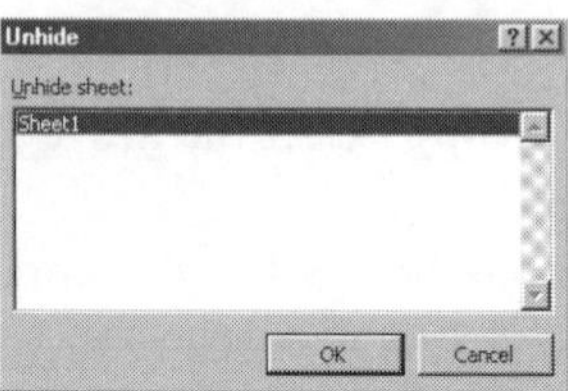

Figure 5.5 View a hidden worksheet.

Naming, grouping and ungrouping worksheets

To name a worksheet, right-click on its tab, then select **Rename** (see Figure 5.6). Type the new name and press on the **Enter** key.

You can display up to 31 characters for the name of your worksheets. It is better however not to go overboard: the tab would take up too much space!

You can group worksheets to speed up work. In fact, grouping worksheets is the equivalent of inserting carbon paper between worksheets: everything you enter and format on the first worksheet is faithfully reproduced on the other worksheets in the group.

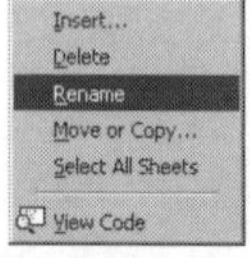

Figure 5.6 Renaming a worksheet.

To group several worksheets, click on the first tab of the group, keep the **Ctrl** key pressed, then click on the other tabs you wish to group.

To ungroup worksheets, click on one of the tabs which is not grouped.

■ Data

Before starting your calculations, you must enter various data. Data for a worksheet are numbers, legends and formulas.

Types of data

Excel allows the insertion of several types of data (see Figure 5.7):

- **Numbers.** Raw data which Excel needs. These numbers are entered in cells.
- **Legends.** Text which you type at the top of a column or at the start of a row to specify its contents.
- **Formulas.** Entries which indicate to Excel which are the calculations to be carried out. For example, the =A2-A5+B8 formula indicates to Excel that it must add cell A2 and B8, then subtract cell A5.
- **Functions.** Predefined formulas which execute more complex calculations with a single operator. For example, the Average function calculates the average for a set of values.

Excel applies a different alignment to cells according to the nature of the inserted data. Therefore, text is left-aligned in the cell which contains it while a number is right-aligned, as are functions, dates and formulas.

Figure 5.7 Excel allows you to enter several types of data.

Entering data

To enter data, click on the relevant cell. A black frame will be shown around the cell, to indicate that it is selected. As soon as you start entering data, it is displayed in the active cell and in the Formula bar (see Figure 5.8). Click on the **green box** in the Formula bar to confirm the entry and insert it in the cell (you can also press the **Enter** key). Click on the **red X** to undo your entry (you can also press the **Esc** key).

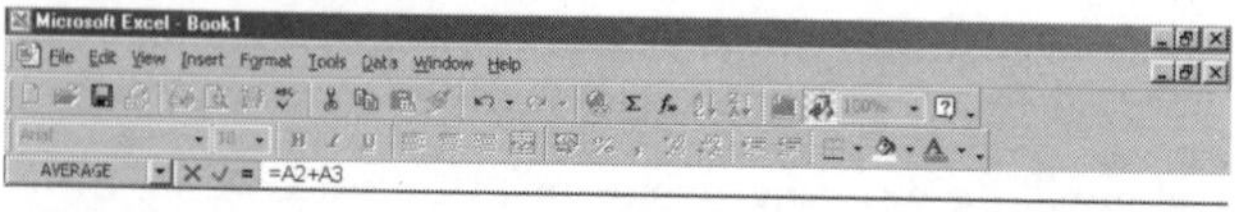

Figure 5.8 You can insert, confirm and delete data in the Formula bar.

*If your entry does not fit into the cell, when you confirm the entry the content is cut if it is text, or displayed as asterisks if it is a number. To fit the column automatically to its contents, click on **Format**, **Column** and select **AutoFit Selection**.*

To edit the contents of the cell in which you are entering your data, use the **Backspace** key or the **Del** key, then type your correction. To edit the confirmed entry once, double-click on the cell, then implement your correction. You can also click on the cell and edit its contents in the Formula bar.

Special data

As we have already said, text is left-aligned, a value (number, function or formula) is right-aligned. However, in some cases you may wish to insert numbers as text (for example, a postcode). In such cases, you must instruct Excel that this is text by left-aligning it. Before starting your text entry, press the **apostrophe** (') key.

On the other hand, a date or a time, though it is text, must be considered as a value because it may be used for calculation purposes. To insert date or time values in a worksheet, enter them in the format you wish to be displayed (see Table 5.1).

Table 5.1 Various date formats

Entry	Outcome
DD/MM	1/1 or 01/01
DD/MM/YY	1/1/99 or 01/01/99
MMM-YY	Jan-99 or January-99
DD-MMM-YY	1-Jan-99
DD-MMM	1 January
DD Month YYYY	1 January 1999
HH:MM	17:15
HH:MM:SS	10:25:59
DD/MM/YY HH:MM	25/12/99 13:15

Selecting

These are the various selection procedures:

- To select a cell, click on it.
- To select a row, click on its number in the row header.
- To select a column, click on its letter in the column header.
- To select the whole worksheet, click on the greyed button at the intersection of a row header with a column header.

Cell range

Often you may need to select the same group of cells several times. To speed up the task, you can create a cell range:

- For a range with contiguous cells, click on the first cell, then drag the mouse to the last cell in the range.
- For a range with non-contiguous cells, click on the first cell, keep the **Ctrl** key pressed, click on the second cell, and so on.

To name a range:

1. After selecting a range, click on the reference, which is on the left-hand side of the Formula bar (see Figure 5.9). Type the name following these rules:
   a. The range name must start with a letter or an underlining hyphen.
   b. The range name must not be the reference for any cell.
   c. Do not use space between characters or digits.
   d. Use the underlining hyphen to separate two words.
   e. Type a maximum of 255 characters.
2. Press the **Enter** key.

Once you have named your range, to select it you simply click on **Edit, Go To** and specify the range you want (see Figure 5.10).

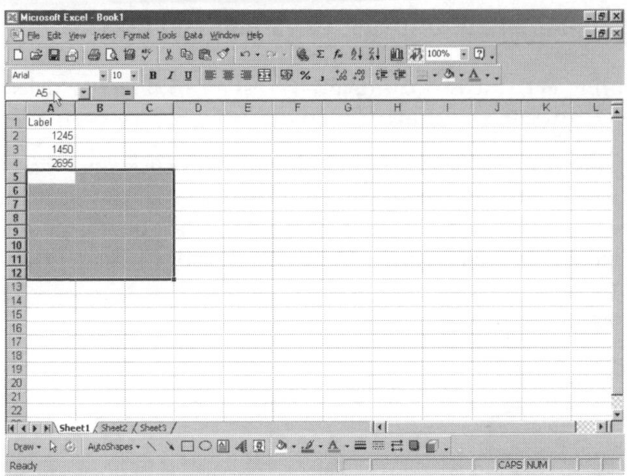

Figure 5.9 Naming a cell range in the reference box.

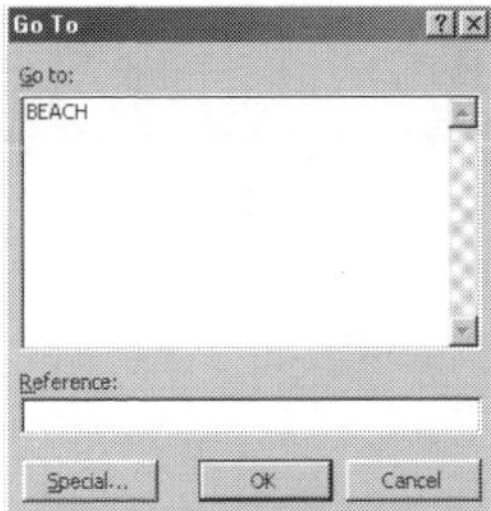

Figure 5.10 Selecting a range in the Go To dialog.

■ Management of cells, rows and columns

During entry, it is occasionally necessary to insert or delete cells, rows and columns.

To insert a cell, a row or a column, right-click on the cell before or after the place you wish to insert the new element, then select **Insert, Cells** (see Figure 5.11). Click the choice you require (**Shift cells right** or **Shift cells down**). Click on **OK.**

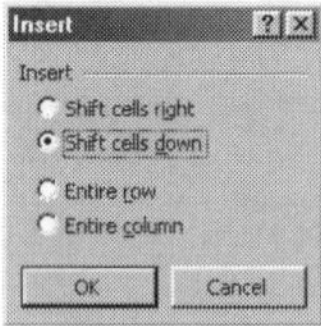

Figure 5.11 You can insert cells, rows and columns using the Insert dialog.

To delete one or more blank cells, rows or columns, after having selected them, right-click on the selection, then select **Delete.** You can also click on **Edit, Delete** (see Figure 5.12). Select your choice from the list, then click on **OK.**

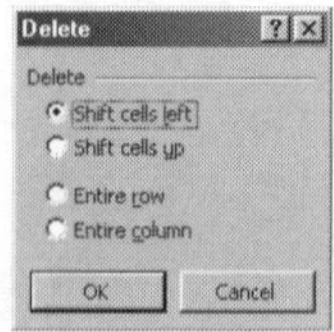

Figure 5.12 With the Delete dialog, you can delete cells, rows and columns.

To delete only the text or the values from one or more cells, after having selected them, press the **Del** key. The cells are kept, but their contents are deleted. On the other hand, when you wish to delete the contents of formulas, but not the format or the comments, and so on, after having selected them, click on **Edit**, **Clear**, then select the appropriate option in the pop-down menu.

Remember that:

- **Contents** clears text from the cell.
- **Format** clears the format, but keeps the existing text.
- **Comments** clears the comments.
- **All** clears the set of choices defined above.

Help with your entry

Excel offers several functions for helping with entering data which allows you to work faster.

Fill

When you must insert the same label into several cells, or the same value or even the same date, use the **Fill** function.

To fill a value, a date or a label in the same worksheet:

1. Drag your mouse on the cell which contains the entry for the fill, then on those to which you wish to apply the fill. Click on **Edit**, **Fill**.
2. Select the direction for the fill – **Down**, **Right**, **Up**, **Left** (see Figure 5.13).

   Excel fills the selected cells with the contents of the first cell.

*To copy one or more cells, you can also use the **Copy**, **Paste** or **Cut** buttons in the Standard toolbar.*

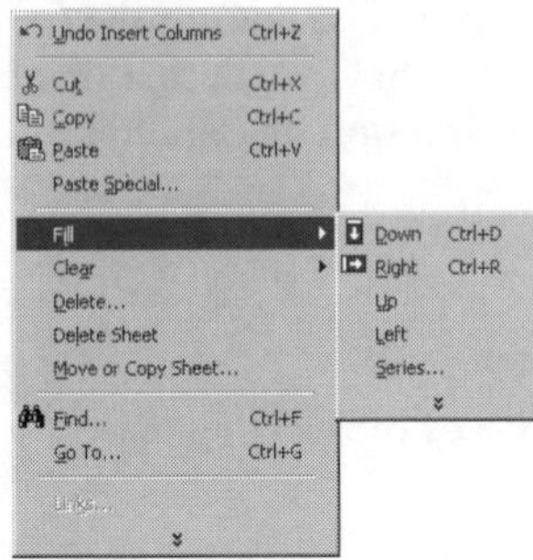

Figure 5.13 The Fill command.

Fill handles

To fill a cell, you can also use the fill handle (see Figure 5.14). Before using this handle, make sure you are aware of all its different uses.

- A fill handle will be shown in a row header when you select it. Drag it to fill the contents of the row. Repeat this procedure in a column header to fill the whole column.
- To insert blank columns, rows or even cells, press the **Shift** key, then drag the fill handle.
- Drag the fill handle with the right button to display its context menu.

To use a cell fill handle, click on the relevant cell: a little square is displayed on the bottom right corner: this is the fill handle. Click on it, then drag it on the cells to be filled.

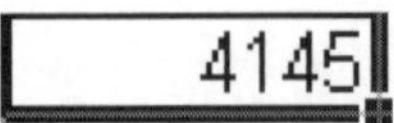

Figure 5.14 Fill handles.

According to the contents of the cell, Excel executes different types of fill:

- The cell contains a numerical value: Excel fills this value.
- The cell contains, for example, a month: Excel inserts the following month, in sequence.

This function corresponds to inserting a series. Excel offers several integrated series in AutoFill. You can create your own fill series.

To create an automatic fill series:

1. Click on **Tools**, **Options**, then on the **Custom List** tab. If required, click on **NEWLIST** in the list on the left. Type the new list and click on the **Add** button.
2. Click on **OK** to confirm your automatic series.

Format

Excel offers several possibilities for formatting a table. You have the same choice of attributes (font, bold, italic, and so on) offered in Word. See Chapter 3 to get to know them. You will find here formats which are specific to Excel.

AutoFormat

To use **AutoFormat:**

1. Select the table. Click on **Format, AutoFormat** (see Figure 5.15).
2. Select the format in the **AutoFormat** list.
3. If you wish to modify one of the default format attributes, click on the relevant check box in the **Options** box, then carry out your changes and click on **OK**. Again, click on **OK** to confirm the format you have selected.

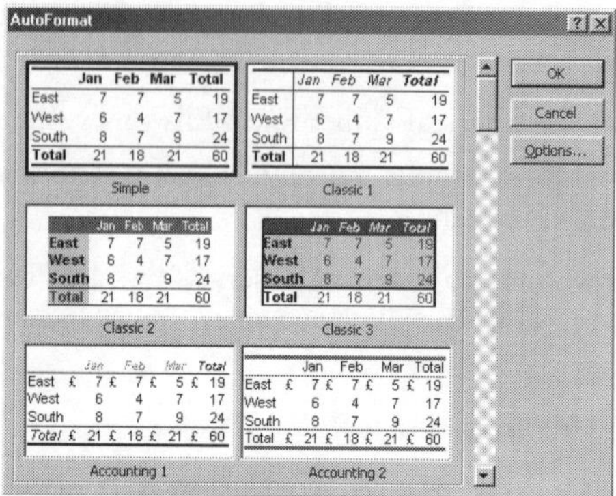

Figure 5.15 Choose AutoFormat.

Conditional formatting

Conditional formatting allows you to apply a format according to specific criteria. For example, you wish the cell containing the profit to be displayed in a different colour if it is a negative amount, which will allow you to spot immediately 'the size of the trouble'.

To create a **Conditional Formatting:**

1. Select the relevant cell. Click on **Format, Conditional Formatting.**
2. In the second option of the **Condition 1** box, select the parameter to be applied.
3. In the third option of the **Condition 1** box, type the value. Click on the **Format** button.
4. In the **Color** option, select the colour, then click on **OK** (see Figure 5.16). Click on **OK** again.

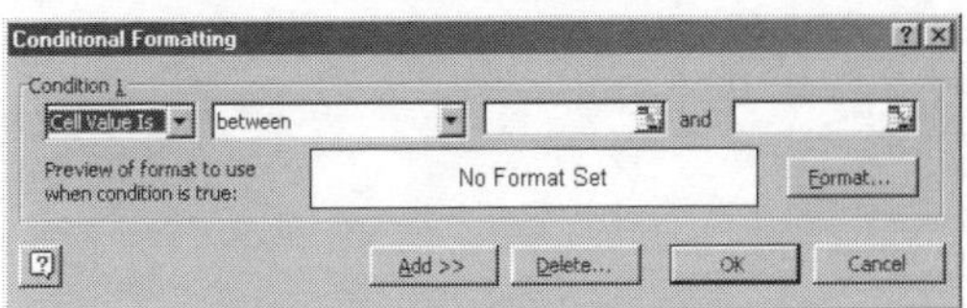

Figure 5.16 The Conditional Formatting dialog allows you to define a conditional format for certain cells.

6 Advanced Excel functions

Formulas

Functions

Scenarios

Sorting and filtering data

Auditing

Creating a chart

Here we will be using advanced Excel functions such as creating formulas, using functions, sorting data, and so on.

Formulas

A formula allows simple arithmetical operations, such as addition or subtraction, to be carried out using the various data in the worksheet.

Before you start, get to know the various operators used and their order of priority in terms of their application:

- all operations in brackets;
- raising numbers to n-power;
- multiplication and division;
- addition and subtraction.

Remember this order of priority and always bear it in mind when creating calculation formulas, otherwise you could end up with the wrong results.

Creating formulas

To create a formula:

- The formula is inserted into the cell which will contain the results.
- A formula always starts with the equals sign (=).
- A formula uses the reference of each cell included in the calculation. For example: =A1_B5.
- A formula may use numbers. For example: =4*5.
- A formula uses one or all of the following symbols: + to add, - to subtract, * to multiply, / to divide, and an exponent to indicate an n-power.

To create a formula with numbers:

1. Select the cell which will display the results of the formula. Press the = key, then type the formula.
2. Press the **Enter** key to confirm the formula or click on the **green box** in the Formula bar. Excel calculates the result and displays it in the originally selected cell.

To enter a formula with cell references:

1. Select the cell which will display the results of the formula. Press the = key.
2. Click on the first reference cell for the formula and press the arithmetical operator. Click on the second reference cell, and so on. Repeat this procedure for each cell in the formula.
3. When you have finished, press the **Enter** key to confirm the formula (see Figure 6.1) or click on the **green box** in the Formula bar.

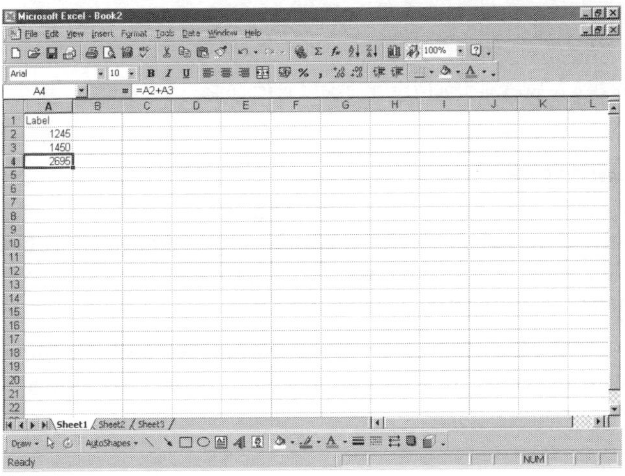

Figure 6.1 A formula in Excel.

With the created formulas, Excel executes calculations and enters the outcome in the appropriate cells.

*Automatic calculation, in the context of formula creation, slows down the processing of the worksheet. If you wish to deactivate it, click on **Tools**, **Options**, then on the **Calculation** tab and finally on the **Manual** option (see Figure 6.2). Confirm with **OK**.*

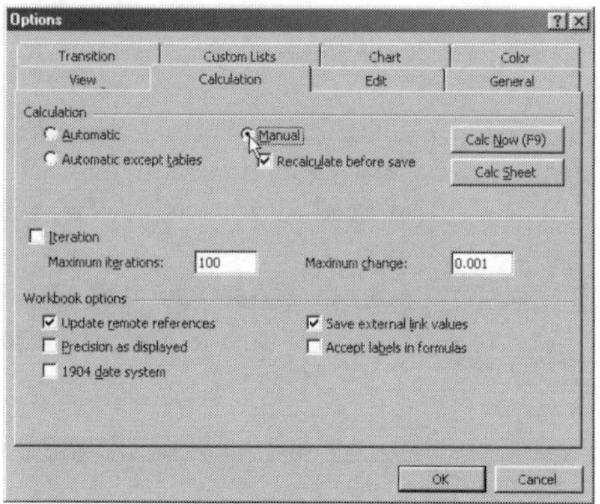

Figure 6.2 You can deactivate automatic calculation.

Converting into euros

With an eye on the difficulties Europeans will encounter when they switch to the euro, the programmers of Office 2000 have developed a tool which allows you to convert currencies into euros quickly and easily.

To use the EuroConverter, in the relevant cell click on **Tools**, **EuroConverter** (see Figure 6.3). Confirm the conversion and click on **OK**.

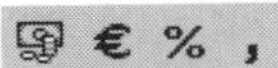

Figure 6.3 Click on the euro currency symbol on the toolbar to convert to and from the euro.

Copying and moving formulas

When you copy a formula from one point in the worksheet to another, Excel adjusts the references to the new position. For example, when you copy cell C11 which contains the formula =SUM(C4:C10) and you insert it in D11, this displays =SUM(D4:D10). If you do not want Excel to adapt references and want instead to keep the initial cell references, you must give the instruction that the referenced cells are fixed and should not be modified. You must therefore mark up each reference cell as an absolute reference. Press the **F4** key immediately after having typed the reference. A dollar icon is displayed in front of the letter and number of the reference (for example D11).

If you do not wish to use the F4 function key, type the **$** *sign in front of each reference letter or number.*

■ Functions

Excel offers a number of predefined functions. They are available to carry out a series of operations on several values or on a range of values. For example, to calculate the average quarterly turnover, you can use the @AVERAGE function (A6:D6).

Each function contains three distinct items:

- The @ sign marks the beginning of a formula. Therefore, if you type the = sign, Excel will replace it automatically with @.

- The name of the function, AVERAGE in our example, indicates the type of operation to be carried out.
- The argument, A6:D6 in our example, indicates the reference cells on whose values the function must operate. The argument is often a cell range. This could be an interest rate, a sorting order, and so on.

There are three types of arguments: database, criteria and field arguments. The first two refer to cell ranges and the last to a column label.

Wizard function

If it is true that you can enter functions yourself, as well as their arguments, Excel is fully aware that this could be boring. To make this task easier, the Wizard Function will assist you and will make creating these functions much easier.

To use Wizard Function:

1. Click on the cell in which you want to insert the function. Click on **Insert, Function.**
2. Select the function category of your choice in the **Function category** list. Select a function in the **Function name** list. A description of the function selected is displayed in the lower part of the box. (see Figure 6.4)

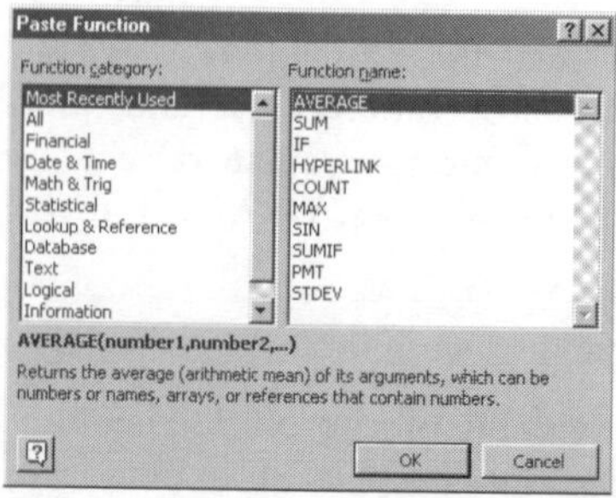

Figure 6.4 Use the Insert Function Wizard to create your functions quickly.

Click on **OK** to confirm your function. A dialog box is displayed for the selected function.

3. Work through the options bearing in mind the instructions displayed in the lower part of the box. Click on **OK** or press the **Enter** key. Excel inserts the function as well as its argument in the selected cell and displays the results.

Automatic entry

When processing a worksheet, the most frequently used function is working out a total.

To obtain the total of a row or a column, click on the cell at the edge of the row or the column. Click on the **AutoSum** button. In the cell, the range of the column or the row is displayed. Press the **Enter** key or click on the **green box** to confirm (see Figure 6.5).

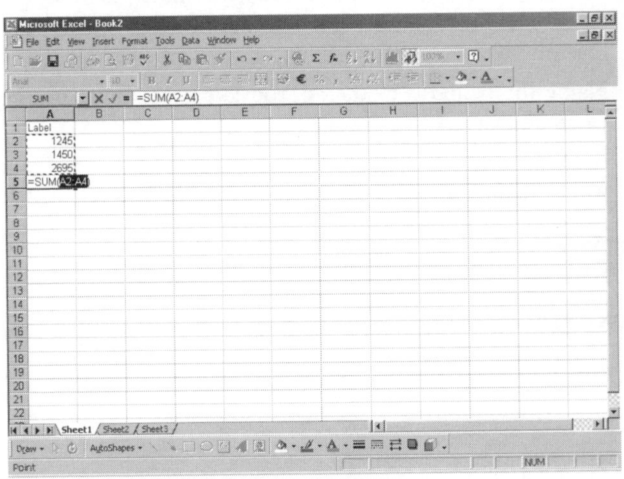

Figure 6.5 Clicking the Sum button allows you to add the contents of a column or row.

*When you use the **AutoSum** function, the cell range you wish to add must not contain blank cells.*

■ Scenarios

Scenarios allow you to create calculations based on theoretical values and to determine their effects on the results. Let us take a simple example: you are a writer and you wish to work out your potential royalties if you sell 500, 5,000 or 10,000 copies of your book.

Creating a scenario

You can create a scenario with a few clicks:

1. In your worksheet, click on **Tools, Scenarios**. The Scenarios Manager is displayed and indicates that the worksheet does not contain a scenario. Click on the **Add** button.
2. Name the scenario in the appropriate area. Click on the **Changing Cells** option (see Figure 6.6).
3. In the worksheet, click on the cell in front of the one which will contain the scenario (in our example, the cell which

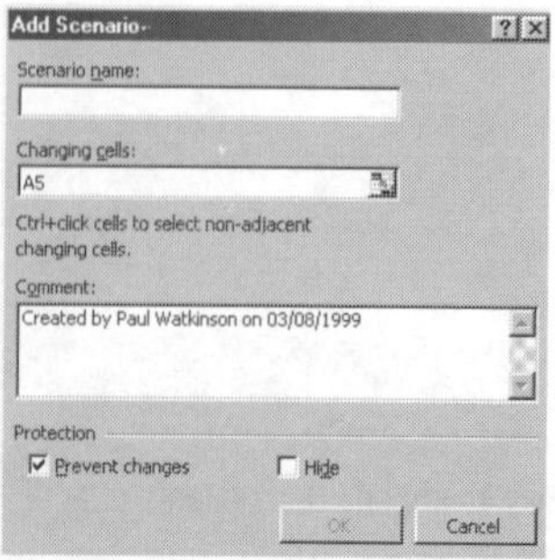

Figure 6.6 The Add Scenario dialog allows you to specify in exactly which cell you want your scenario.

contains the total sales). If you wish to modify several cells for the scenario, select each one by separating them with a semi-colon. Click on **OK** to confirm your cells. The **Scenario Values** dialog box displays the values shown in the cells to be edited.

4. Type the values to be used for the scenario, then click on **OK**. For our example, you should enter 500 and 5,000. The Scenarios Manager displays the name of the scenario you have just created.
5. To display the results of a scenario, click on its name, then on the **Show** button.

Sorting and filtering data

Once you have finished inserting functions and formulas, you can use some Excel tools which allow you to manage, sort and filter data.

Sorting data

When you type data, it is rare that you follow specific criteria. You must therefore sort your data as follows.

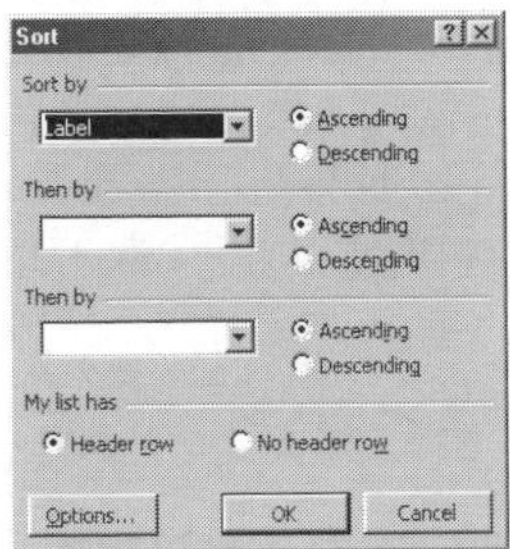

Figure 6.7 You can specify how you want your data sorted in the Sort dialog.

1. Select the cells range you wish to sort. Click on **Data, Sort** (see Figure 6.7). Select the sort criterion in the **Sort by** box.
2. If required, select a second sorting criterion in the **Then by** box. Click on the option corresponding to your choice for each criterion (**Ascending** or **Descending**).
3. Specify whether the table contains a header or not in the **Header row** box. Click on **OK**.

*To sort a column quickly, you can use the **Ascending** or **Descending** buttons in the Standard toolbar.*

Filtering data

When the worksheet contains several rows or columns, you can view only the ones on the screen. To access specific data, you can use the **Find** function (see Chapter 1), but this function is too complex for this type of search, and allows access only to specific data. The **Filtering** function allows access to any data within a few seconds.

You cannot use the Filtering function if the table does not contain a column header.

To create automatic filtering:

1. Click on one of the cells, then on **Data, Filter, AutoFilter**. Each column header displays an arrow (see Figure 6.8).
2. To implement a sort, click on the arrow in one of the headers, then select the filtering criteria to be used. Excel displays row numbers and the arrows of the headers of filtered data in blue.

Figure 6.8 By clicking on the arrow in one of the headers, you can select the filtering criteria to be used.

*To delete a filter, click on the arrow in the relevant header, then on **All**.*

To customise the filter:

1. Click on the arrow of the header for which you wish to customise sorting, then select **Custom**.
2. Define the first filtering criterion in the area with the name of the column, then specify the second filtering criterion, if you need to, after having ticked the appropriate option (**And**, **Or**). Type the cell, the date, the town, the client, and so on, then click on **OK** (see Figure 6.9).

*To deactivate AutoFilter, click on **Data**, **Filter**, **AutoFilter**.*

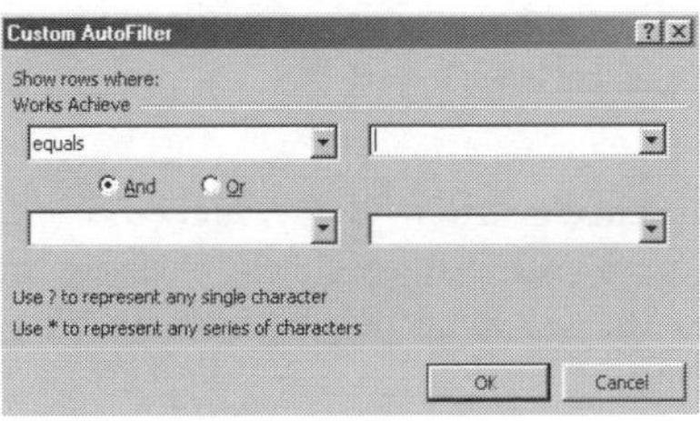

Figure 6.9 You can also create custom filters.

■ Auditing

Excel offers several auditing tools which allow you to check dependencies between cells and therefore to avoid any mistake. Once you have used the various auditing buttons proposed in the toolbar of the same name, it is guaranteed that the results are correct.

To implement an audit:

1. Click on **Tools**, **Auditing** (see Figure 6.10).
2. Select the type of auditing to implement.

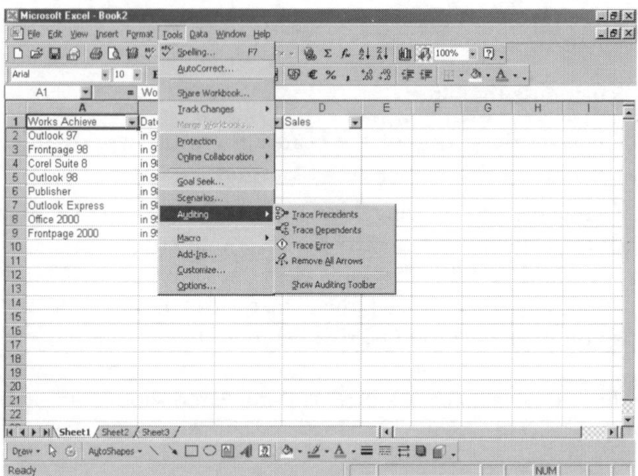

Figure 6.10 Select the type of auditing to implement.

To implement the various checks, after having clicked on the cell whose interdependencies you wish to check, click on the button corresponding to the verification you wish to carry out in the Auditing toolbar.

■ Creating a chart

To simplify the task of creating a chart, Excel puts a Wizard at your disposal.

To start the Chart Wizard:

1. After having selected the data you wish to use for your chart, click on the **Chart Wizard** button.

   a. **Chart Type.** Lists the various charts which you can implement.

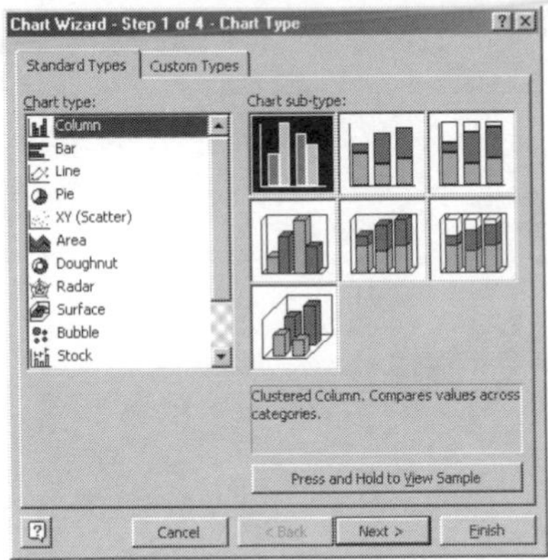

Figure 6.11 Select the type and sub-type of the chart you want.

   b. **Chart sub-type.** Displays the sub-types available for the type of chart selected. The description of the selected sub-type is displayed underneath this list.

2. Click on the type of chart to be applied. Click on the chart sub-type. The **Press and Hold to View Sample** button allows you, by clicking on it and keeping it pressed all the time, to view the chart you are creating. Click on the **Next** button (see Figure 6.11).

   a. **The Data Range tab.** Allows you to modify the range previously selected and to specify the position of the data (see Figure 6.12).

   b. **The Series tab.** Allows you to edit, add or delete a series.

3. After having carried out your modifications, click on the **Next** button. This step allows you to create settings for one or more items in the chart. The dialog box has several buttons you can use for your editing: Titles, Data Table, Axes, Legend, Data Labels, and so on (see Figure 6.13).

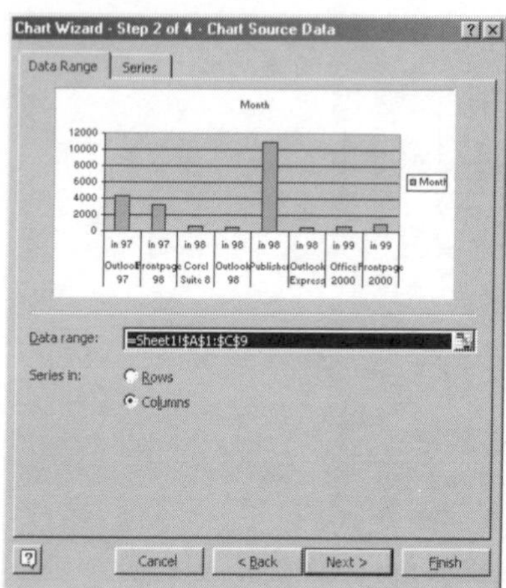

Figure 6.12 The second step of the Chart Wizard is to select the source data.

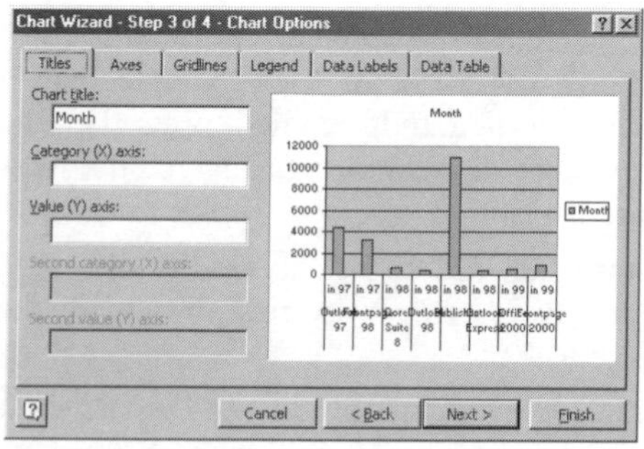

Figure 6.13 The third step of the Chart Wizard is to choose the options you want for Titles, Data Table, Axes, Legend, Data Labels, and so on.

4. After having carried out your modifications in the various tabs, click on the **Next** button. This final step allows you to specify the address for the chart (see Figure 6.14).

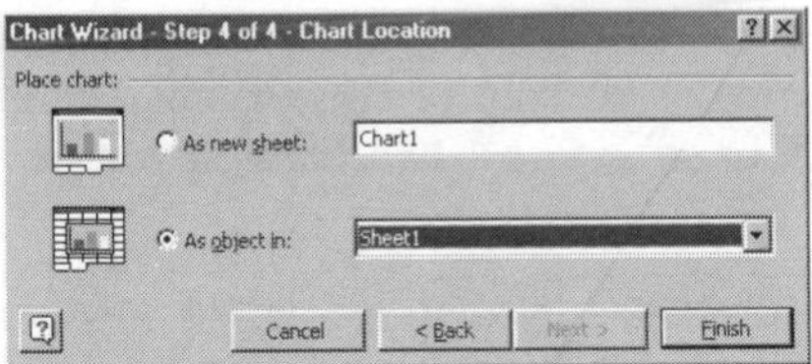

Figure 6.14 The fourth and final step of the Chart Wizard is to choose the location of the chart.

a. **The As new sheet option.** Allows you to add a worksheet chart to your workbook. If you choose this option, remember to enter the name of the new worksheet.

b. **The As object in option.** Allows you to insert the chart in the worksheet where you have selected the data. So this is an embedded object, but independent. You can easily move it or resize it, because it is not linked to the cells in the worksheets.

5. Once you have defined these options, click on the **Finish** button.

According to the options in the fourth step, the chart is inserted into a chart worksheet or into the active worksheet.

To select a chart, click on it. Around the chart, Excel displays small squares known as *handles*.

To move the chart, click on the chart, then, keeping the button pressed, drag it to where you want to place it and release the mouse button.

To reduce or enlarge a chart, click on one of the handles, then drag to achieve the size you want.

Editing a chart

Excel offers several options to control the aspect and the functioning of a chart. To edit a chart, Excel puts at your disposal several tools:

- **Chart menu.** Available when the chart is selected. It offers options which allow you to edit the type, to select other data, to add, and so on.
- **Context menu.** Available with a click of the right mouse button on any object in the chart.
- **Chart toolbar.** Allows you to edit format, objects, type, legend, to display the data table, and so on (see Table 6.1).

Implement the required modifications using various buttons.

Table 6.1 Buttons in the Chart toolbar

Button	Action
Chart Area	Displays the list of the items in the chart. By clicking on the item of your choice in this list, you select it.
	Opens a dialog box which offers formats to be applied to the selected item.
	Chooses another type of chart.
	Displays or hides a legend.
	Activates or deactivates the data table which displays the data in the chart.
	Shows the data selected by row.

Button	Action
	Shows the data selected by column.
	Angles text downward, from left to right.
	Angles text upward, from left to right.

7 Basic PowerPoint functions

The first step

Display views

New presentation

Text

Harmonisation

Formatting slides

Pictures

Charts

In this chapter, we will study the basic functions of PowerPoint such as opening a new presentation, formatting, and so on.

The first step

When you start the program, the PowerPoint dialog box is displayed (see Figure 7.1). From this dialog box, you can choose a number of options:

Figure 7.1 The PowerPoint dialog allows you to choose how to create a new presentation.

- **AutoContent Wizard.** Allows you to launch a Wizard which, through a number of steps, will allow you to create a presentation quickly.
- **Design Template.** Allows you to select a theme, a background, a predefined presentation, animation, and so on.
- **Blank presentation.** Allows you to open a blank presentation.

- **Open an existing presentation.** Allows you to display a previously created presentation.

*If the PowerPoint dialog box is not displayed, click on **Tools, Options**. Click on the **View** tab. Tick the **Startup dialog** option, then click on **OK** to confirm.*

Converting a presentation

You can open a presentation created in another program. Click on the **Open** button in the Standard toolbar. In the Files of type box, select the application in which the required document was created. Double-click on it in the list which is displayed. PowerPoint automatically converts the presentation so that it can be modified.

Applying a template

You can renounce a format by changing it to a predefined template.

To apply a template to an already created presentation:

1. Click on **Format, Apply Design Template** (see Figure 7.2).
2. Select a template, then click on **Apply**.

AutoContent Wizard

When you require a presentation quickly, use the AutoContent Wizard:

1. Click on **AutoContent Wizard** in the PowerPoint dialog box. If this dialog box is not active, click on **File, New**. Click on the **General** tab. Double-click on the **AutoContent Wizard** icon. Click on **Next**.
2. In the second step (see Figure 7.3), you can choose the presentation type. PowerPoint offers a number of themes to cater for most business needs. Press a category button (list on the left) for the type of presentation you are going to

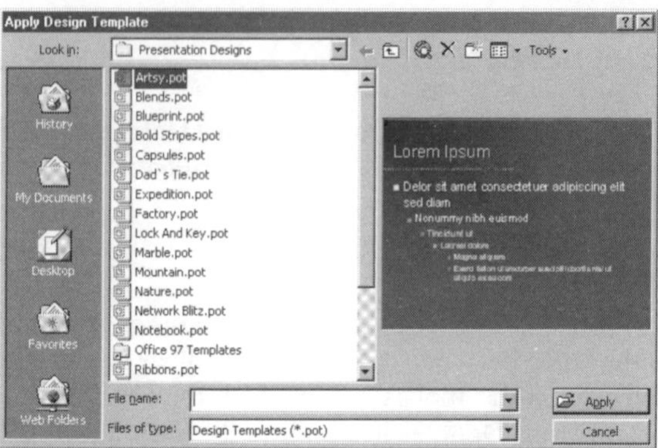

Figure 7.2 You can apply a template to a presentation that has already been created.

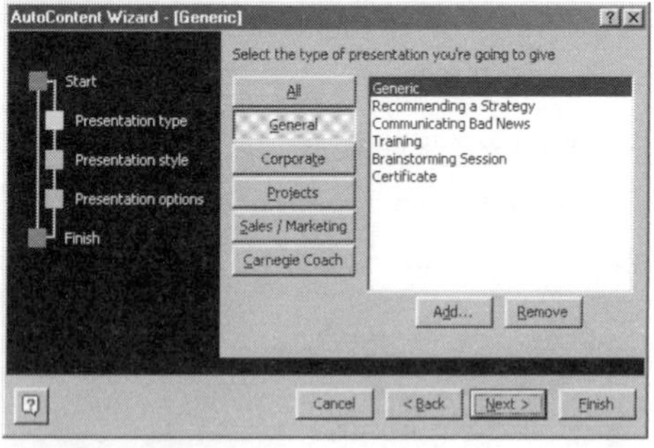

Figure 7.3 Choosing the presentation type.

give and then select the presentation that best fits your needs (list on the right). You can add one of your own presentations by choosing a category and then pressing **Add**. Click on **Next**.

3. You must now select the type of output for your presentation. Click on **Next**.

4. You can specify the presentation title, the contents of the footer, the slide number, and so on. Click on **Next**, then on **Finish**.

Display views

PowerPoint offers several ways for viewing a presentation. Each view allows a different type of intervention:

- **Normal.** As a new feature in the 2000 version, you have a three-sided view: on the left, an Outline view, in the centre, a Slide view, and, at the bottom, a view that corresponds to the old Notes view. This allows you to work on the presentation structure, contents and notes all at the same time (see Figure 7.4). This is the default display view.
- **Outline.** Allows you to view, in its most important part, the slides by title level: the text of the various slides on the

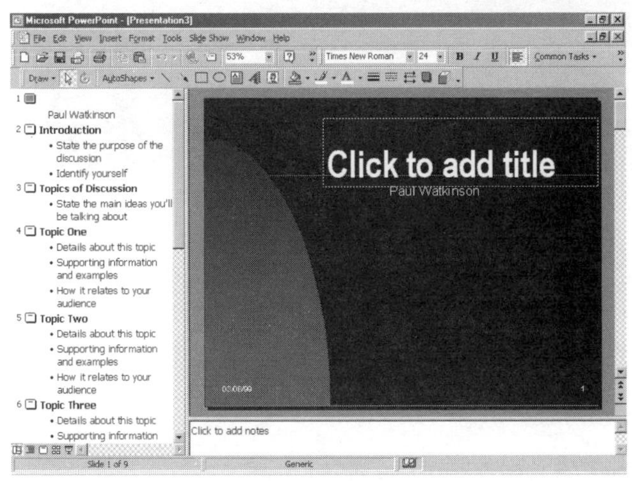

Figure 7.4 Slide view in Normal viewing mode.

left, a small preview of the slide in the right-hand corner, and a window to insert notes (see Figure 7.5). In this view, you can work on the presentation contents and organise the flow chart which creates a logical sequencing for the various slides. To navigate between slides, double-click on the title of the slide you wish to display.

- **Slide View.** Allows you to view a slide at a time. This is the view where you can insert text, add objects (sound, charts, pictures), and so on.
- **Slide Sorter View.** Allows you to view on screen all the slides in your presentation. This is the ideal view to sort slides, move them, copy them, and so on.
- **Slide Show.** Allows you to view the set of slides in sequence. In this view, the slide takes up the whole screen. This is where you can test the actual show and the animation effects you may have created.

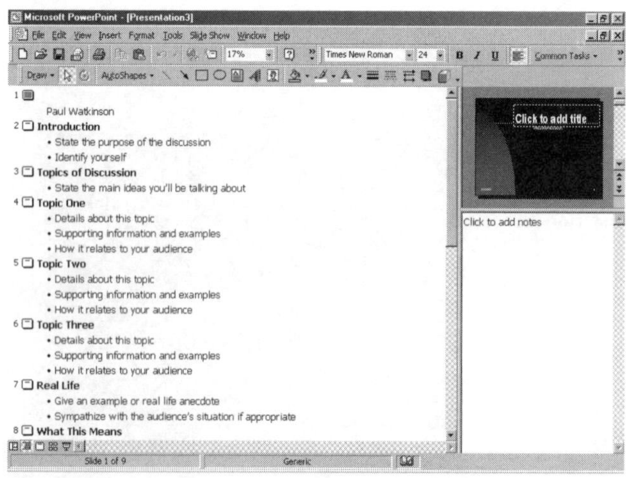

Figure 7.5 Slide view in Outline viewing mode.

To change view, click on the appropriate display button in the bottom left corner of the window (see Figure 7.6). You can also click on **View**, then select a display view.

If you wish to enlarge or reduce any part of a slide, click on **View, Zoom**. Choose the zoom percentage (see Figure 7.7).

Figure 7.6 Viewing mode buttons.

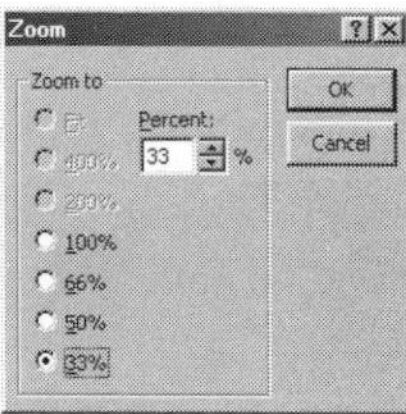

Figure 7.7 You can use the Zoom dialog to change the view on screen.

■ New presentation

Let us now see how to create a new presentation for which you will create the format yourself:

1. Click on **Blank presentation** in the PowerPoint dialog box or on **File, New**. Click on the **General** tab, then double-click on the **Blank presentation** icon.
2. In the New Slide dialog box, choose the type of slide to be created (see Figure 7.8). Click on one of the types to select it. The right side of the box displays a textual description of the selected type. Click on **OK**. The number of the slide is displayed in the status bar (slide X of X).

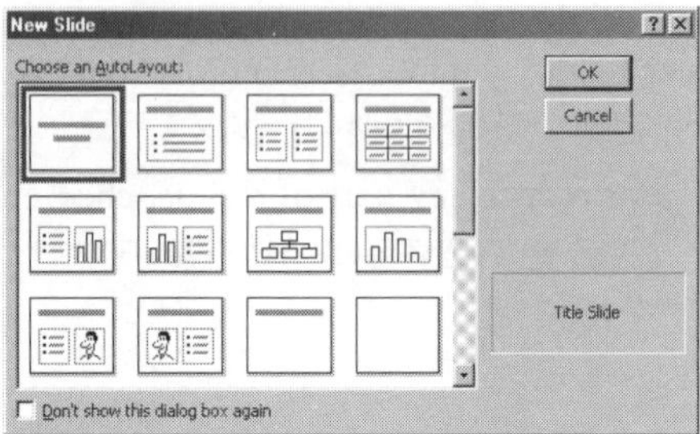

Figure 7.8 You can choose between AutoLayouts in the New Slide dialog.

Inserting, deleting and formatting slides

A presentation rarely contains a single slide. You must therefore know how to insert, delete or format slides.

- To delete a slide, display it in Outline view or Slide Sorter view, then click on it and press the **Del** key.
- Insert slides by clicking on the **New Slide** button. Select the type of slide as explained above and click on **OK**. PowerPoint inserts the new slide and assigns the previous format to it.

  You can also click on **Insert, New Slide** or, in the Format toolbar, on the **New Slide** icon. Repeat the above procedures to choose the type of slide.
- When you have chosen a type of slide but you are no longer happy with it, you can change it. Click on the **Common Tasks** button and select **Slide Layout** (see Figure 7.9). Select the new type, then click on **Apply**.

Moving between slides

These are procedures you need to follow to move between the various slides of the presentation:

- To navigate between slides in Normal view or in Slide view, click on the up or down double-arrow in the vertical

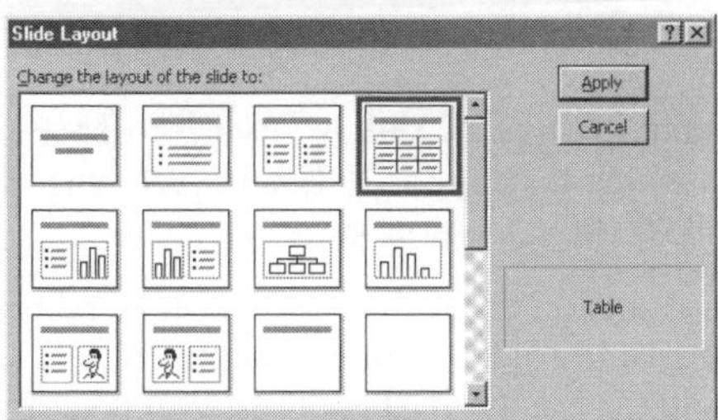

Figure 7.9 You can change the layout of your slide in the Slide Layout dialog.

scroll bar. You can also drag the scroll bar. A balloon displays the number of pages while you are scrolling. Release when you get to the slide you wish to display.

- To navigate between slides in Outline view or Slide Sorter view, click on the slide to be selected (see Figure 7.10).

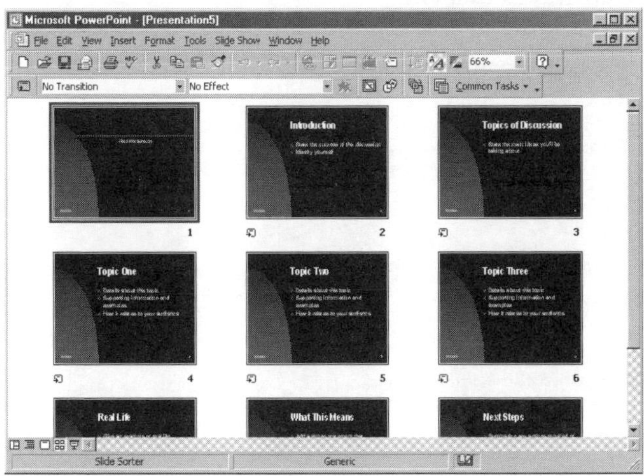

Figure 7.10 Move quickly between slides in the Slide Sorter.

Text

Once you have selected the type of slide you wish to create, you must start by inserting text into it. Whatever the type of slide chosen, you follow the same procedures:

- To insert text, you must click on one of the text boxes which reads **Click to add...** The frame around the text box becomes greyed and the pointer flashes. Type your text. To exit from the text box, click outside it. You can write whatever you want as you would do in a text processing program, the line feed is therefore automatic.

In PowerPoint 2000, the text automatically fits the frame.

To activate Auto-fit text:

1. Click on **Tools, Options,** then on the **Edit** tab (see Figure 7.11).
2. Tick the **Auto-fit text to text placeholder** option to activate it. Click on **OK.**

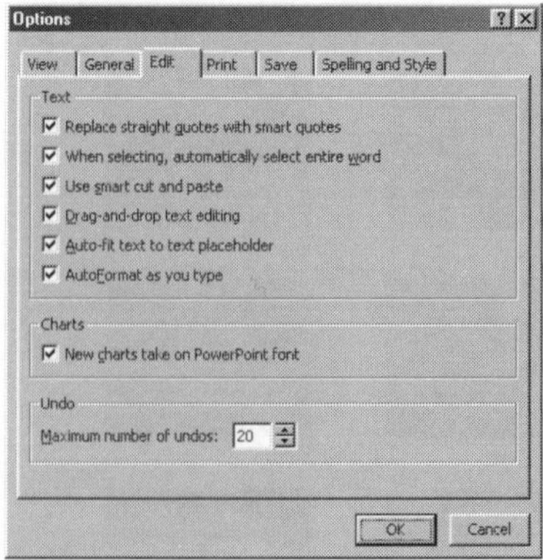

Figure 7.11 Activating the Auto-fit text.

The function which allows the text to fit automatically to the text frame is not active for titles.

*To insert a text box, click on the **Text Box** button in the Drawing toolbar and draw the frame in the slide.*

Selecting text

For any editing or deleting operation, you must know how to select the text on which to act. These procedures are explained later in the book.

Bulleted lists

A bulleted list is a set of structured topics which can be positioned at various levels. This type of presentation for text is extremely practical, because it allows each topic to be displayed point by point. To display a slide of this type, click on the **Bulleted list** template in the New Slide dialog box.

The bullet is the icon which is displayed to the left of each topic. Type the text in the area which contains the bulleted list, then press the **Enter** key each time you wish to display a new bullet. By default PowerPoint displays small round black bullets.

To create a bulleted list, you can also select a text, then click on the **Bullets** button in the Formatting toolbar.

*To change a bulleted list to normal text, select the list, then click on the **Bullets** button to deactivate it.*

If you no longer want the default bullets, change them:

1. In the bulleted list, press the **Ctrl+A** keys to select the entire bulleted list.
2. Click with the right mouse button on the selection, then select **Bullets and Numbering** (see Figure 7.12). Click on the type of bullet to select it. You can modify the colour

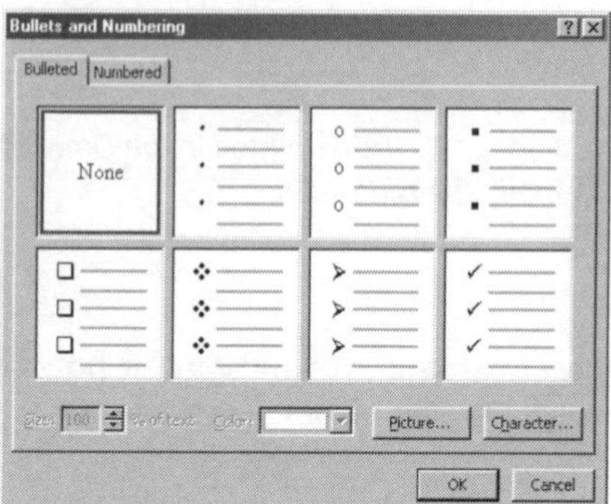

Figure 7.12 Selecting a different bullet style in the Bullets and Numbering dialog.

and the size of the bullet in the **Color** and **Size** options. The **Character** button allows you to select a letter or any other icon as a bullet. Click on **OK**.

Now, PowerPoint allows you to use a ClipArt picture as a bullet. In the **Bullets and Numbering** dialog box, **Bulleted** tab, click on the **Picture** button. In ClipArt, click on the bullet of your choice, then on OK.

■ Harmonisation

PowerPoint allows you to harmonise presentations thanks to its masters and its colour schemes.

Slide Master

The Slide Master controls font, size of characters for all titles, bullet lists, sub-titles, and so on, and contains the charts shared by all the slides. It also allows you to insert date, slide number, and any other information you may wish to include.

To display the Slide Master for a slide, click on **View**, **Master**. In the pop-down menu, select **Slide Master**. Then, follow the instructions below to use or edit the Slide Master:

- To edit titles, select the master title, then use the **Font** and **Size** drop-down list. For more complex modifications, use the Font dialog box; to open it, click on **Format**, **Font**.
- To edit the text in bulleted lists, select the bulleted list in the master, then use the **Font** and **Size** drop-down list. You can use other buttons in the Formatting toolbar such as the **Font Size** arrow.

Slide Master controls all aspects of slides. When you edit an area in the master, the modifications apply to all the slides in the presentation. If you wish this format not to apply to one of the slides, display it in Slide view, then click on **Format**, **Background**. In the dialog box which is displayed, tick the **Omit background graphics from master** option to activate it, then click on **Apply**.

Colour scheme

Each predefined template offers a different colour for each of the items in slides: titles, bulleted lists, numbered lists, fill, and so on. You can easily modify the colour for each category of items as follows:

1. Click on **Format**, **Slide Color Scheme** (see Figure 7.13).
2. In the dialog box which is displayed, you can choose a standard scheme or create a custom colour scheme. It is better, however, to use a standard scheme to avoid problems (ill-assorted colours and so on). If you do not like any of the standard colour schemes, click on the **Custom** tab, then select a colour for each element of the slides. Once you have completed your choice, click on **Apply to All** so that the colour scheme applies to the whole presentation or click on **Apply** so that it applies only to the selected slide.

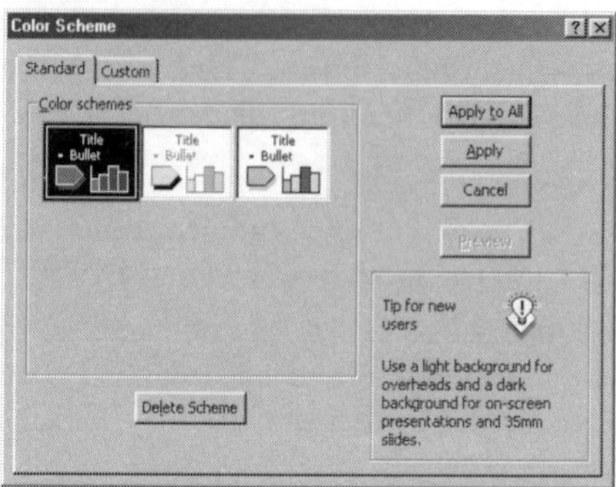

Figure 7.13 Colour Schemes allow you to harmonise your presentation.

■ Formatting slides

Just as in Word, you can create a custom format.

Some tips for formatting text

To format text, you must first select it as explained earlier in this chapter. To select all the text in a slide in Outline view, click on its icon. In Slide view, simply press the **Ctrl+A** keys.

For text, formatting options are the same as in Word (see Chapter 3). Here we provide some hints and tips:

- **The Slide Master view.** Allows you to modify the appearance of text for all slides. To give coherence to the format, carry out the modifications in the master.

If you have added text boxes to some slides, the master cannot control them.

- **The Slide view.** Displays the various slides of the presentation one by one. To assign the text of a slide a different aspect from the master, carry out your modification in this view, because it allows you to see the text exactly as it will appear in the Slide Show.

- **The Outline view.** Displays only the text. This view allows you to display the text effect of each slide and compare it to the others. It is ideal if you wish to modify the font or the character size for the whole text in all the slides of the presentation. Click on **Edit**, **Select All**, then select the required font. You can also use the various buttons in the Format toolbar.

Background

Each slide has a background, coloured or not according to the way you have created the slide.

To modify the background:

1. Click on **Format, Background** (see Figure 7.14).
2. To choose a colour for a background, click on the arrow in the **Background fill** pop-down list, then choose the colour. To choose another colour, click on the **More Colors** button, then choose a colour or specify it yourself. The **Motifs** option in **Fill Effects** allows you to select a gradient, a texture, a pattern or a picture for the background. Click on **OK**.

Figure 7.14 Choosing a background colour.

■ Pictures

Pictures are obviously very attractive when producing a slide show, because they support the presentation and explain visually – and therefore more immediately – the contents of any slide.

PowerPoint allows you to insert several types of pictures:

- Digital pictures, produced with a scanner or a digital camera.
- Vector pictures produced with image-creation programs such as Illustrator. They are created from mathematical shapes and are made up of basic elements: lines, regular areas, and so on.
- Pictures from the Office ClipArt Gallery.

Remember that a digital picture may be either in black and white, or in grayscale, or in colour.

To insert a picture, follow the procedures in Chapter 2.

Picture toolbar

The Picture toolbar allows you to retouch a picture. This is displayed automatically when you select a picture (by clicking on it) and offers buttons for editing contrast, brightness, cropping, display in colours or black and white, and so on. Refer to Table 7.1 to see how to use these buttons.

Table 7.1 The buttons in the Picture toolbar

Button	Action
	**Insert Picture from File.** Inserts an existing picture in the active file at the insertion point.
	**Image Control.** Changes a picture colour to grayscale, black and white or as a watermark (a transparent image which appears under the text without hiding it).
	**More Contrast.** Increases the picture contrast.
	**Less Contrast.** Decreases the picture contrast.
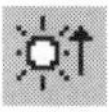	**More Brightness.** Increases the picture brightness.
	**Less Brightness.** Decreases the picture brightness.
	**Crop.** Trims or restores portions of a picture. Click on this icon, then drag a sizing handle on the picture.
	**Line Style.** Modifies the lines framing the picture.
	**Recolor Picture.** To enable this command, select a single picture or OLE object.
	**Format Object.** Defines formatting options for the picture.
	**Set Transparent Color.** Makes one of the colours in the picture transparent.
	**Reset Picture.** Restores the picture to its original status.

■ Charts

When preparing your presentations, you will often need to present series of figures to show the progress for a product, the structure of your client list, the distribution of a set of items, and so on. In this situation the audience does not have a great deal of time to try to understand and analyse figures. To help overcome this problem, add a chart which will allow your audience to come to grips with the figures you are introducing and to make your point clearly and forcefully.

If you have either created your slides with AutoContent Wizard or have selected a slide predefined for charts, simply double-click on the **Double-click to add chart** message. If you have chosen a blank slide or if you wish to insert a chart in a text slide, you must click on the **Insert, Chart** button in the Standard toolbar.

Whichever procedure you use, the PresentationNumber – Datasheet window is displayed with data as examples.

To enter the data you wish to format, click on the cell you want, type the data, then press the **Enter** key to confirm. You must use the direction keys to move within the table cells. By default, data are arranged by rows. Columns titles are displayed on the horizontal axis (X) in the chart. If you want a disposition by columns, with rows titles on the X axis, click on the **By Column** button in the Standard toolbar.

Refer to Chapter 6 for further information on the creation and modification of charts.

An OLE is special inter-program technology you can utilise to share information between programs. All Office programs support the OLE technology.

8 Advanced PowerPoint functions

Placing objects

Drawing

Style coherence

Sorting, structuring and adapting slides

Animation

Starting a slide show

Slide show on paper, on slides or other media

Speaker notes

Transferring a slide show

In this chapter, we will examine advanced PowerPoint functions such as drawing, placing objects, organising a slide show, and so on.

■ Placing objects

When you place some items (pictures, text, or others), you have several methods for placing them precisely.

Ruler and Guides

To place an object exactly, the Ruler and the Guides are indispensable.

To activate the Ruler, click on **View**, **Ruler**. When you drag the object, a dotted line will appear in the ruler, showing the exact position of the object edge. Release when you are exactly where you want to be (see Figure 8.1).

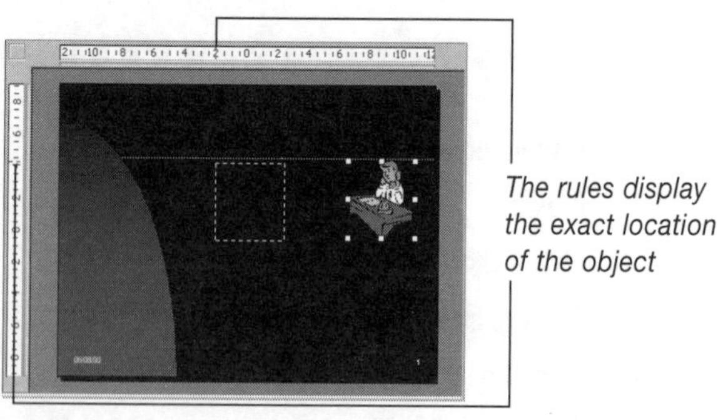

Figure 8.1 You can place objects exactly with the Ruler.

To activate the Guides, click on **View**, **Guides.** On the screen you will see a dotted cross. When you drag an object onto a guide, the object sticks to it. To move a guide, click on it, then

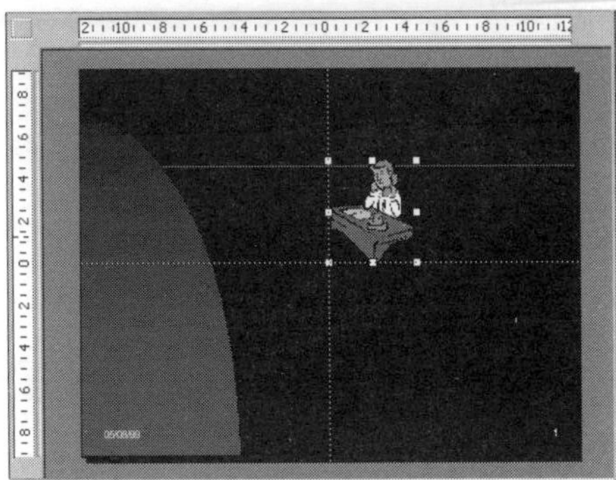

Figure 8.2 The Guides help you to position two objects exactly.

drag it to where you want to be. You can therefore align objects on the slide with absolute perfection (see Figure 8.2).

Arranging objects

While you are creating your slide, you pile up objects on the slides ... and you end up no longer being able to see the objects in the background. If you wish to modify one of the hidden objects, you must 'bring it back to the fore'. If it is still visible, click on it; otherwise, click with the right mouse button on one of the objects of the pile, then select **Order.** In the submenu (see Figure 8.3), click on the choice you want:

- **Bring to Front.** Places the selected object on top of the pile.
- **Send to Back.** Places the selected object at the bottom of the pile.
- **Bring Forward.** Brings the selected object forward by one place.
- **Send Backward.** Sends the selected object backward by one place.

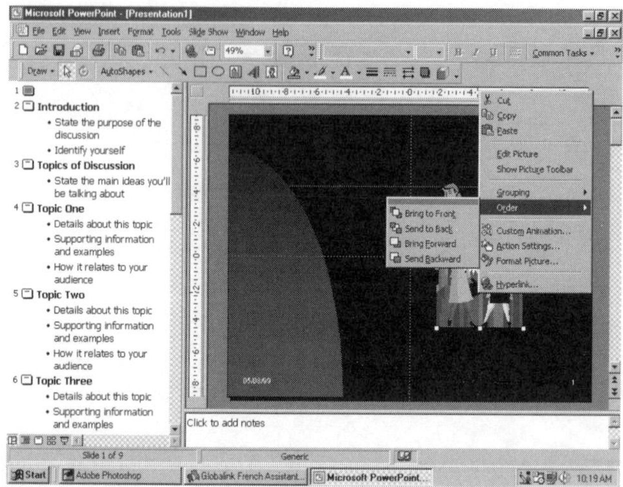

Figure 8.3 The options available for organising your objects.

■ Drawing

With PowerPoint you can insert shapes and arrows, and you can draw and create tables for your presentations.

Drawing toolbar

The various drawing tools are available in the Drawing toolbar at the bottom of the screen. You can draw lines, shapes and arrows or even select AutoShapes. Simply click on the tool, then insert it into the slide. Use the various buttons to add colour, modify the line style, and so on.

Creating tables

To create a table for a presentation, you no longer need to insert it from another application: click on **Insert, Table** (see Figure 8.4). Define the number of columns and rows for the table, then click on **OK**.

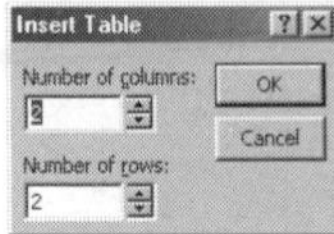

Figure 8.4 Inserting a table into a presentation.

To insert new rows or new columns, use the pointer which has become a pencil and draw.

All the procedures to move between cells, to insert text, modify the colour, and so on, are identical to those used for tables in Word. See Chapter 4.

■ Style coherence

PowerPoint offers a tool for checking the style of the presentation and its coherence.

To activate the checking of the style:

1. Click on **Tools**, **Options**, then on the **Spelling and Style** tab.
2. In the Style area, tick the **Check style** option box (see Figure 8.5). Click on **OK**.

To define the style to be used:

1. In the Spelling and Style tab, click on the **Style Options** button (see Figure 8.6). The two tabs, **Case and End Punctuation** and **Visual Clarity**, give you all the options you need for your checks.
2. Specify the options required, the title text size, the title case, the sentence case, and so on. Click on **OK** to confirm.

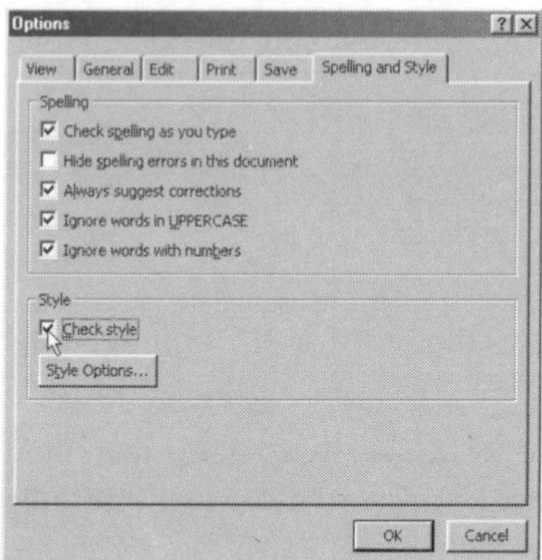

Figure 8.5 Activating Check style.

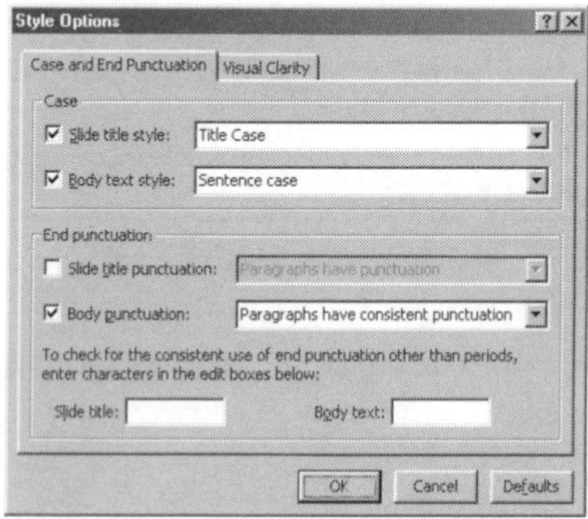

Figure 8.6 Setting the Style Options to achieve the desired style coherence.

Now, if the presentation you have produced has any discrepancy according to the style you have defined, PowerPoint warns you in a dialog box which brings all the problems to your attention.

Sorting, structuring and adapting slides

To make your slide show perfect, you must sort the slides. The best way to do this is by using the Slide Sorter View which will allow you to reorganise easily the set of your slides and sort them. Click on the **Slide Sorter View** button, at the bottom left of the screen (see Figure 8.7).

To copy a slide:

1. Click on the slide and press the **Ctrl** key.
2. Keeping this key pressed, drag – a vertical line is displayed and follows the drag. It indicates where the copy is going to be inserted when you release the key.

To move a slide, repeat the above procedure without pressing the **Ctrl** key.

To delete a slide, click on it, then press the **Del** key.

To move slides, you can also use the Outline view. In this view, all slides are first reduced to their title level. You can then move them by dragging their icon up or down in the outline. A horizontal line is displayed and moves as you move, showing where the slide will be placed when you release the mouse button. You can also move the slide with the **Up** or **Down** buttons in the Outlining toolbar.

Organising a slide show with the summary slide

When you create a slide show to be shown on a computer or on the Web, you can use as a starting point a summary slide which contains a bulleted list with the titles of all the slides in the presentation (it is a sort of table of contents). When you start the slide show, you can therefore choose the direction you wish to follow from the summary slide.

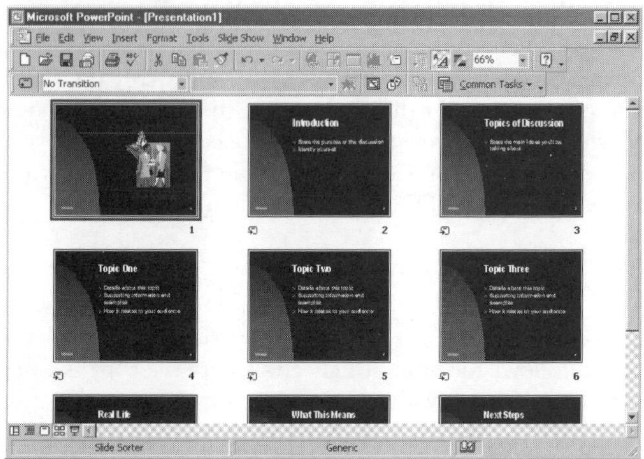

Figure 8.7 Slide Sorter.

 To create a summary slide:

1. In Slide Sorter View, click on the first slide in the Slide Show which the Summary Slide should include.
2. Press the **Shift** key, then click on the second slide, and so on, keeping the key pressed.
3. Click on the **Summary Slide** button in the Slide Sorter View or Outlining toolbar (see Figure 8.8).

The summary slide becomes the first slide in the presentation. It displays the list of all the selected slides.

 *Refer to Chapter 1 for creating hyperlinks.*

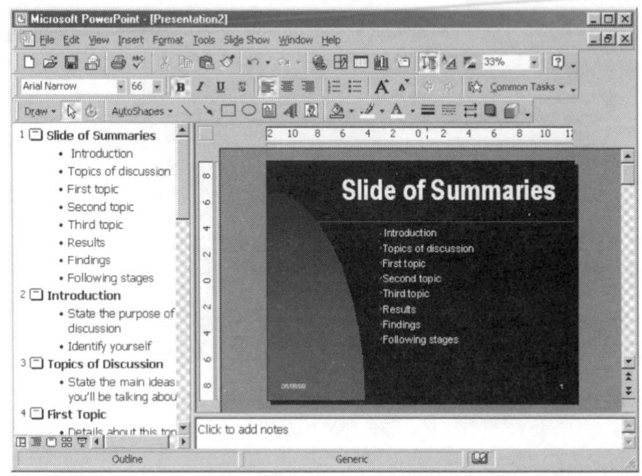

Figure 8.8 The Summary Slide allows you to see the structure of the presentation.

Creating bookmarks

To navigate more quickly in the presentation, you can create bookmarks which allow direct access to the required place when you click on them.

To create a bookmark:

1. In the slide, select the relevant text.
2. Click on the **Insert Hyperlink** button (see Figure 8.9).
3. Click on the **Bookmark** button (see Figure 8.10). Click on the name of the slide you want. Click on **OK** in the two dialog boxes.

Refer to Chapter 1 to discover the new PowerPoint Web functions, which allow you to create automatically a frame sequence in the window to the left of your presentation so that the web surfer can access the slide which is of interest by clicking on that frame.

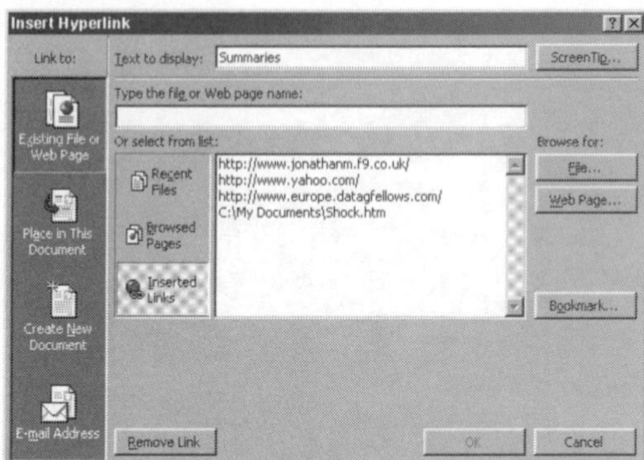

Figure 8.9 Inserting a hyperlink with the Insert Hyperlink dialog box.

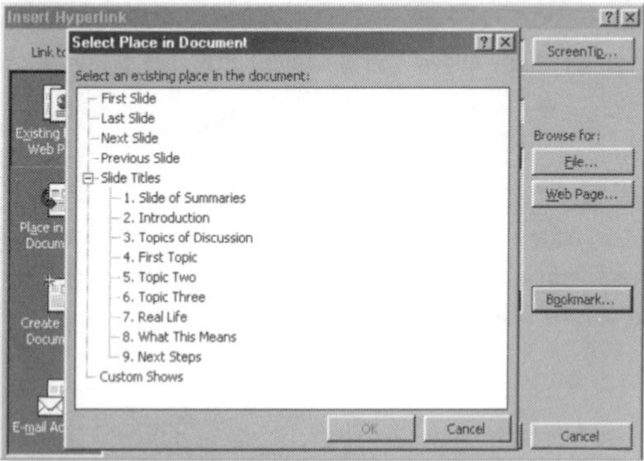

Figure 8.10 Creating bookmarks in a slide.

Narration

PowerPoint allows you to add a sound commentary to the whole slide show. Before starting to record your narration, look at the various buttons and what they do:

- To pause during the slide show, right-click anywhere in the active slide, then click on **Pause Narration.**

- To start recording again, click with the right button, then click on **Resume narration.**

To record a narration:

1. Switch on your computer and check the connection. Click on **Slide Show, Record Narration** (see Figure 8.11). Click **OK.**

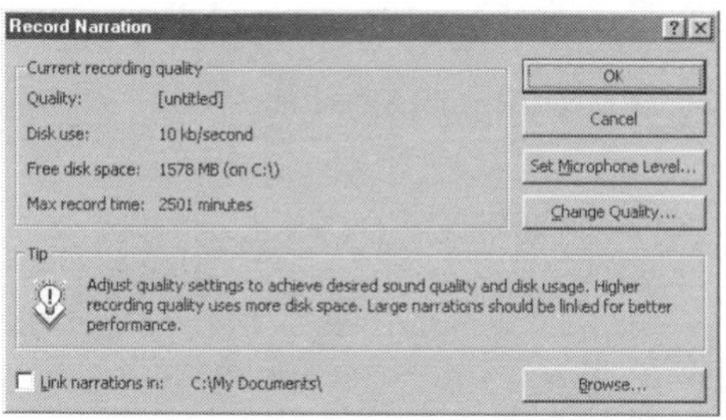

Figure 8.11 Starting the Record Narration function.

2. Click on a slide to move to the following one without interrupting the commentary.

   At the end of the slide show, a message is displayed, asking if you wish to save the slide timings as well as the narrations which have been saved for each slide.

3. To accept, click on **Yes.** To save only the commentary without timings, click on **No.**

When you scroll through the slide show, the commentary is automatically started so that the audience can follow your presentation better.

If you do not want the commentary to start with the slide show:

1. Click on **Slide Sorter View.**
2. Right-click on one of the images and select **Set Up Show.**
3. Click on **Show without narration,** then on **OK.**

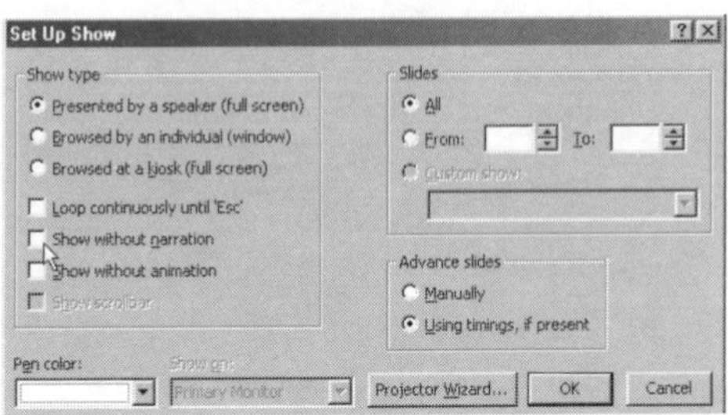

Figure 8.12 Deactivating the Record Narration function.

Adapting the Slide Show to the audience

A slide show may contain information on your company and you may wish to exclude some of this from a general audience. PowerPoint allows you to adapt the slide show according to your audience.

To control a slide show:

1. Click on **Slide Show, Custom Shows**. Click on the **New** button.
2. In the **Define Custom Show** dialog box (see Figure 8.13), name the slide show in the Slide show name option. In the list on the left, click on the first slide to be inserted, then the **Add** button. Repeat this procedure for each slide you wish to insert. To put your slides in a different order, click on the name of the relevant slide in the right-hand window, then on the up or down arrow button.
3. Click on **OK** to save the custom slide show.

Now, to launch the controlled slide show, click on **Slide Show, Custom Show**. Select the slide show you want, then click on the **Show** button to start it.

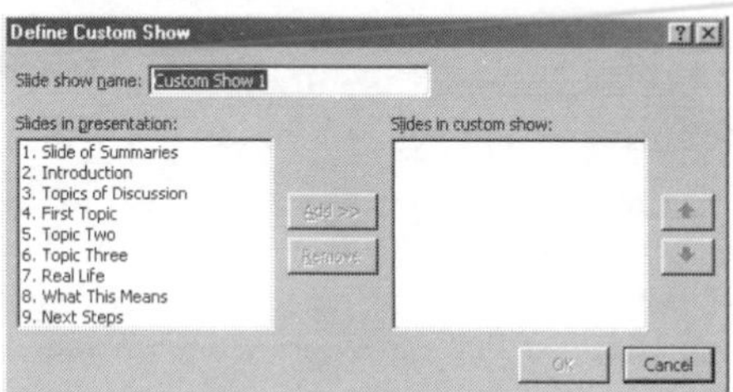

Figure 8.13 Customising your slide show to suit your audience.

■ Animation

We will now go on to a fun function: creation of animation effects.

How to animate transitions between slides

We have all seen, at some time or other, a slide show. Between each slide, the speaker must press a button or click on an icon of some sort to move to the following slide. This technique is not the most efficient because there is usually a lack of synchronisation between the speaker's voice and what you see on screen. With PowerPoint, all these problems are over, because you can time transitions between each slide and create amusing animations.

To manage transitions between slides:

1. Click on the slide to be animated, then on the **Transition** button in the Slide Show menu.
2. Click on the arrow in the **Effect** area, then choose an option. The display area shows the effect of the selected transition.
3. Click on the required option underneath the pop-down list (**Slow**, **Medium** or **Fast**) to define the speed of the transition. In the Advance area, click on **On mouse click** to control

the slides' progression manually or click on **Automatically after** for PowerPoint to automatically display the following slide after the specified number of seconds.

4. To assign sound to the transition, click on the arrow in the **Sound** pop-down list, then select the sound you want. For the sound to last until the following one comes on, click on **Loop until next sound.** Click on **Apply** when you have finished. If you click on **Apply to All**, the specified effects will apply to all the slides.

Slides animation

You can also animate objects (images, text, bulleted list, and so on) in the slide. All these animations are available from the Animation Preview icon in the Animation Effects toolbar displayed in Slide Show:

1. In the relevant slide, after you have displayed it with the Slide Show view, click on the **Animation** button (yellow star) in the Formatting toolbar (see Table 8.1).
2. After having selected the effects you want according to the table shown below, click on the arrow of the **Animation order** option, then specify the order in which the objects should appear on the screen.

Table 8.1 The Animation Effects toolbar buttons

Button	Action
	Animate Title. Activates the animation effects for the title of the slide.
	Animate Slide Text. Activates the animation effects for other texts in the slide.
	Drive-In. Car noise.

Button	Action
	Flying. Makes the object fly.
	Camera. Makes the click of a photo camera.
	Flash Once. Flashes once on the object.
	Laser Text. Displays the text with a laser effect and sound.
	Typewriter Text. Displays the text as if you have been typing on a typewriter.
	Reverse Text Order. Writes the text from bottom up.
	Drop-In Text. Drops the words one by one from the top of the slide.
	Animation Order. Calculates the apparition order of items in the slide.
	Custom Animation. Customises animation.
	Animation Preview. Shows in a small window the selected animation effects.

To create an animation effect, you can also click on the object, then on **Slide Show, Preset Animation.** In the list of proposed effects, select the one you want. When going through the slide show, the chosen effects will appear on the screen with a simple click.

Customising animation effects

PowerPoint allows you to create more targeted animation effects:

1. Click on **Slide Show, Custom Animation** (see Figure 8.14).
2. In the **Check to animate slide objects** area, the various objects of the slide are listed. To select an object, click on it in this area: it will be shown in the Animation order list in the **Order & Timing** tab. In the area to the right of this tab, you can define the **Start animation** options for the selected object. The **Effects** tab allows you to define the effects to be applied to the object. The **Chart Effects** tab allows the slide chart to be animated, and the **Multimedia Settings** tab allows you to define sound effects, animated clips, and so on.

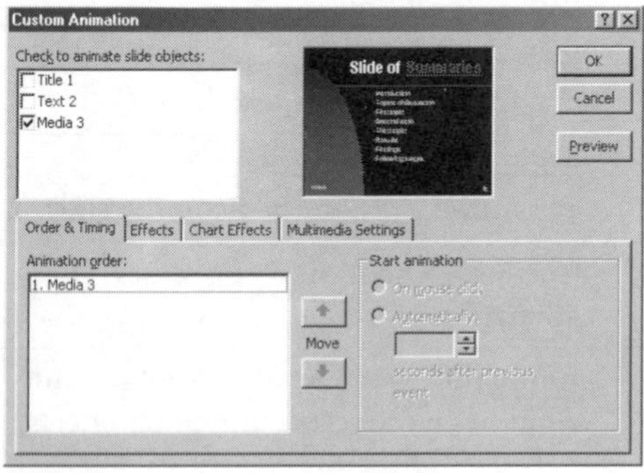

Figure 8.14 Customising the animation of a slide show.

Starting a slide show

Let us now see what the slide show is like and let us check that it works.

To start the slide show, display the first slide, then click on the **Slide Show** button at the bottom of the screen. You can also click on **View, Slide Show**. The slide is displayed on the whole of the screen. To scroll the Slide Show, follow the procedures shown below:

- To scroll the Slide Show slide after slide, click on anywhere in the screen or press the right direction keys at the bottom of your keyboard.
- The Slide Show scrolls automatically if you have defined a specific transition time.
- Press the **Esc** key to exit from Slide Show.
- To display the Slide Show control menu, right-click on the greyed button in the bottom left corner of the slide.
- Double-click on the audio or video clips icon to open them.

Slide show on paper, on slides, or other media

So far, we have seen only a slide show on screen. However, you may not have the latest technology, and therefore do not have the required media. In this case, you must transfer slides on to transparencies, on 35 mm slides or on paper.

To specify the medium you have chosen for your presentation, click on **File, Page Setup** (see Figure 8.15). To adapt your slides to the medium you are going to use, click on the arrow in the **Slides sized for** pop-down list and select the option corresponding to your medium:

- **Letter Paper.** 8.5" × 11" format.
- **A4 Paper.** Corresponds to the traditional 210 × 297 mm.
- **35 mm Slides.** Corresponds to the photo slides format.
- **Overhead.** For overhead projectors.
- **Banner.** For printing on continuous paper.
- **Custom.** Allows you to fit the size of your slides to printer's print area.

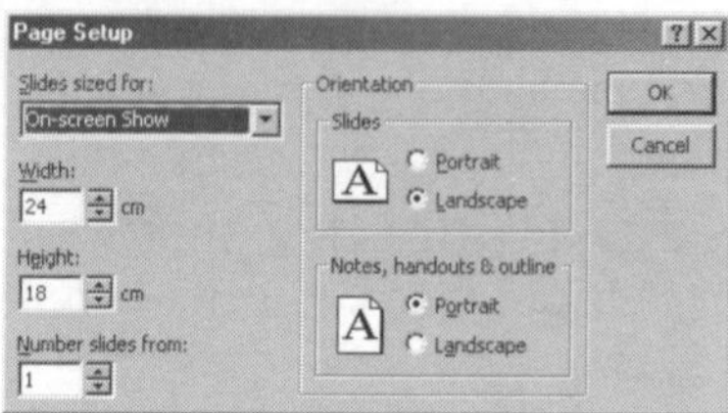

Figure 8.15 The Page Setup dialog allows you to specify the medium you are going to use for your slide show.

You can also change the orientation of your slides which, by default, is Landscape.

■ Speaker notes

To avoid memory lapses during your slide show, it may be better to create some notes. These notes can be entered in the bottom right area in the Normal view.

Inserted notes are not visible to the audience.

■ Transferring a slide show

You may need to transfer your Slide Show, for example if you are doing presentations to all your branches. PowerPoint offers a Wizard which helps you put the whole of your presentation on a diskette, as well as all the files attached to it.

To start this Wizard:

1. Click on **File, Pack and Go**. The Pack and Go Wizard is displayed. Click on the **Next** button to display the second window for this Wizard.

2. Select the presentation you wish to export. Click on the **Next** button to continue. Specify on which type of computer you wish to show your presentation. Click on the **Next** button.
3. You must now include linked files or include TrueType fonts in your presentation. Once you have finished your choice, click on the **Next** button. The Wizard offers to load PowerPoint Viewer in case the computer on which you are planning to install your presentation does not run PowerPoint. Click on the **Next** button, then click on the **Finish** button.

   The Wizard loads your data onto the diskette in your disk drive. You should have several diskettes at the ready, just in case.

9 Basic Outlook functions

In this chapter, we will study the basic functions of Outlook, its main folders, what you can do with them, and so on.

■ Discovering Outlook 2000

With Outlook, you will be able to exchange e-mail, share information with other Office applications and manage a variety of information concerning your activities (appointments, meetings, clients, tasks, and so on).

When you first start Outlook, you may need to configure the installation of Outlook as well as the Internet connection. Follow the step indicated by the Wizard.

The Outlook bar

The Outlook bar, positioned in the left part of the screen, allows you to navigate between the program folders (you will find a description of this further on). If this is not displayed, click on **View**, **Outlook bar**. To display the folder of your choice, click on its shortcut in the Outlook bar: it is displayed in the central window (see Figure 9.1).

Underneath the Outlook bar there are two buttons which allow access to other group bars. To open one of these groups, click on the corresponding button. You need to know that:

- **My Shortcuts** offers folders which help manage, organise and sort your e-mail messages, sent or received.
- **Other Shortcuts** offer quick access to folders or files in another application.

Figure 9.1 The Outlook bar.

■ Outlook Today

This folder lists today's activities and allows access to Messages folders (see Figure 9.2). It is, in a way, a reminder of your activities, of your daily work.

Customize Outlook Today

By default, the Outlook Today folder displays all the tasks to be carried out as well as the contents of your Inbox dialog box. You can customise options for this folder and ask, for example, for it to be displayed automatically when you open the program.

To customise Outlook Today:

1. In the Outlook Today folder, click on the **Customize Outlook Today** option.

2. In the customisation options (see Figure 9.3), specify your choices. When you have finished, click on **Save Changes**.

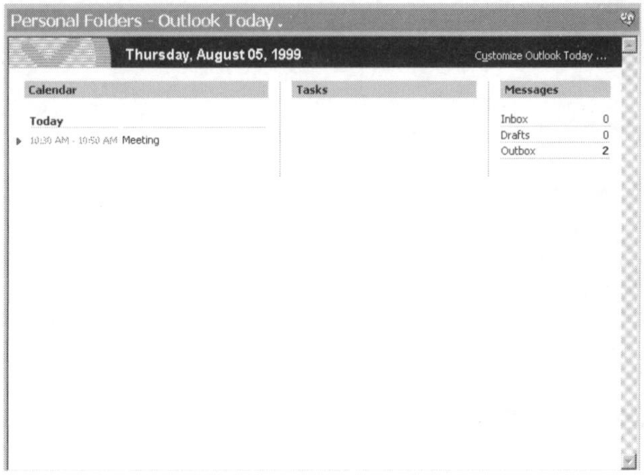

Figure 9.2 The Outlook Today folder.

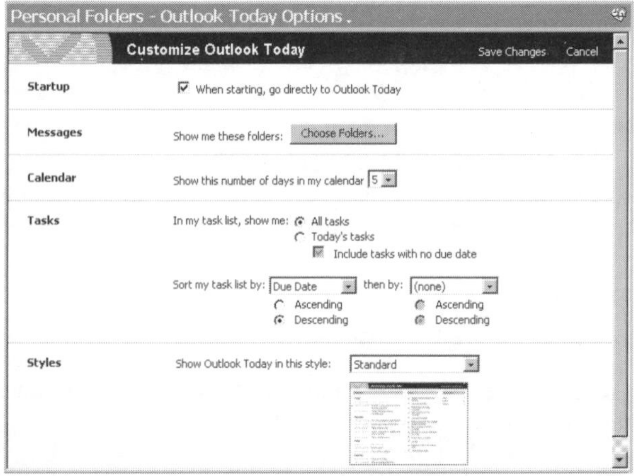

Figure 9.3 You can customise the Outlook Today folder.

Calendar

This folder plans your activities. It allows you to manage your time, note your appointments, plan your meetings, establish a list of your daily tasks, and so on. To display it, click on **Calendar** in the Outlook bar. Calendar offers three main items: Appointments, Dates and TaskPad (see Figure 9.4).

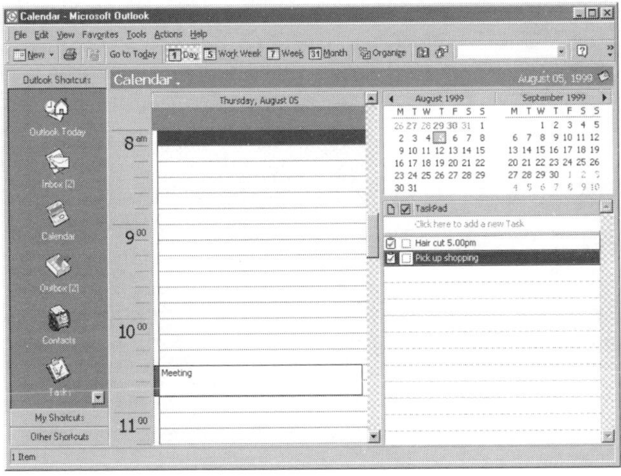

Figure 9.4 Outlook's Calendar folder.

Contacts

This folder is in practice your address book. You will be able to store all your clients' addresses, as well as those of your prospects, your colleagues and also your friends. To display it, click on the **Contacts** icon in the Outlook bar (see Figure 9.5).

If you have a modem, you can quickly dial a telephone number in this folder, send an e-mail message and even go to one

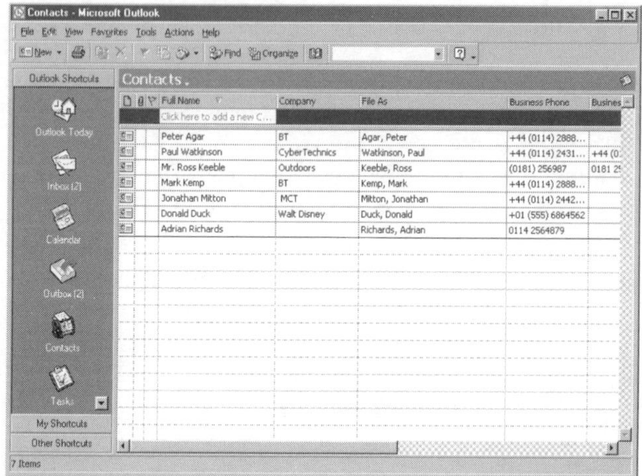

Figure 9.5 The Contacts folder.

of your correspondents' Web pages. To learn how to create contacts or phone one of them, see Chapter 10.

The Contacts folder is your address book. To this effect, it is available to all Office applications to send messages, make a telephone call from an application, and so on.

■ Tasks

A task is a professional or personal mission you need to carry out to its completion (reports, investigations, and so on). The Tasks folder allows you to create various tasks, to follow their status, to assign them to another person, and so on. To display this folder, click on the **Tasks** icon in the Outlook bar (see Figure 9.6).

To familiarise yourself with the procedures for creating, deleting and completing tasks, see page 163.

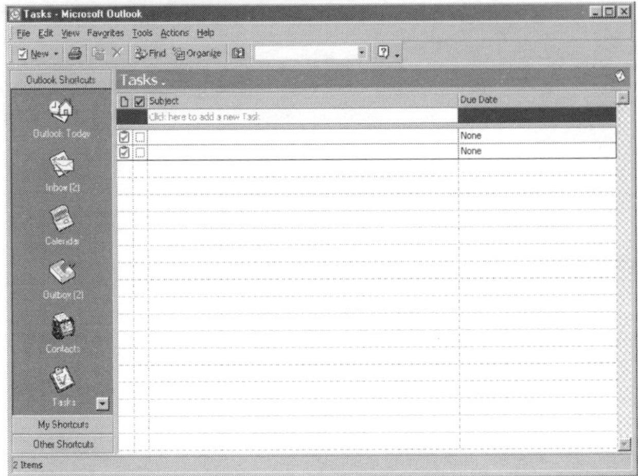

Figure 9.6 The Tasks folder.

■ Journal

This folder is the journal for your activities. You can record here the interaction with your clients, and store items, messages, and so on. You can also create a journal entry without reference to an item. To display this folder, click on **Shortcuts** in the Outlook bar, then on **Journal** (see Figure 9.7).

Creating journal entries

You can create two types of records or entries for your journal: automatic records and manual records.

To create a manual journal entry, without links to any item:

1. Click on the **New** button in the Standard toolbar (see Figure 9.8).
2. In the **Subject** box, type the wording for your entry. Click on the arrow of the **Entry type** option and select the type

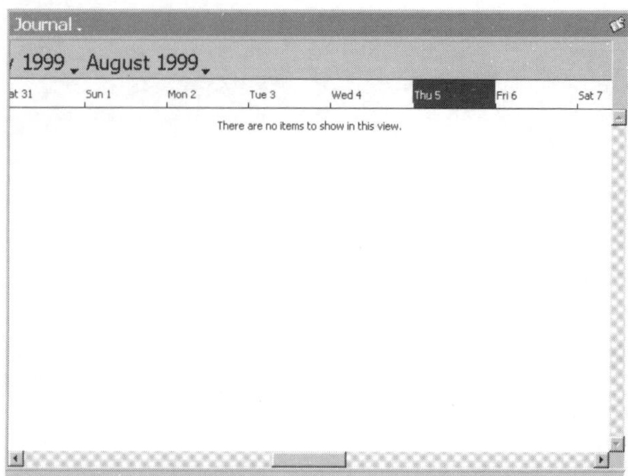

Figure 9.7 The Journal folder.

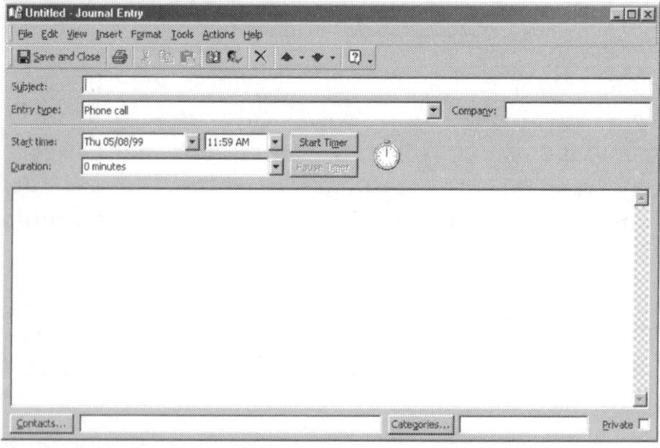

Figure 9.8 Creating a Journal Entry.

you want. In the **Company** box, type, if appropriate, the name of the relevant company. In the **Start time** box, specify the required date. Click on the **Categories** button if you wish to indicate a category. Type your comments in the text box. Click on the **Save and Close** button when you have finished.

In the Journal folder, click on the + icon next to the entry type of your choice to display the list of entries of this type.

To create a manual entry linked to an item:

1. Select the item (contact, task, message, and so on), click on **Tools, Save to journal.**
2. Carry out your modifications as required in the dialog box which is displayed. Click on the **Save and Close** button.

To delete a journal entry, click on it in the list, then on the **Delete** button in the toolbar.

To create automatic journal entries:

1. In the Journal folder, click on **Tools, Options.**
2. In the dialog box which is displayed, click on the **Journal Options** button. Tick the check box of the items you wish to record in the journal. Click on the contact or contacts for which you wish to record elements. If you wish to record in the journal all the elements of an application, click on its check box in the **Also record files from** box. Click **OK.**

   Now, all the activities will scroll in the programs, the contacts or the tasks that you have selected will be recorded in the Journal folder.

*To delete automatic recording of activities, of a contact, and so on, click **Tools**, **Options**, then the **Journal Options** button. Point to the entry type to delete, then click on the right button. Select **Delete** in the context menu which is displayed. Click on **OK** to confirm your deletion.*

Notes

Outlook offers an electronic version of Post-it notes. Use these to jot down your ideas or as a reminder: make notes of things you could use again in your next task or in your next electronic message.

To create a note, click on **Notes** in the Outlook bar. Click on the **New** button, then type the text of the note (see Figure 9.9). When you have finished, click on the **Close** button.

To customise a note, click on the note icon, in the top left corner of the Note window, point to **Color**, then choose a colour.

To open a note, double-click on it. It is displayed on top of all the other Desktop windows. If you change window, the note goes into the background. To find it again, simply click on its button in the taskbar.

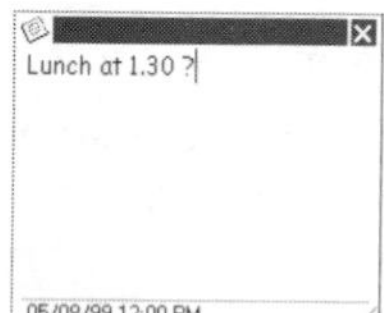

Figure 9.9 A pretty note.

Inbox

The Inbox allows you to organise your e-mail and display received messages (see Figure 9.10). This is the folder which is displayed by default when you start Outlook. It shows the list of messages you have received. To read any message, double-click on it in the list. You can also reply to it and send new messages. You will be able to learn more about this folder in Chapter 10.

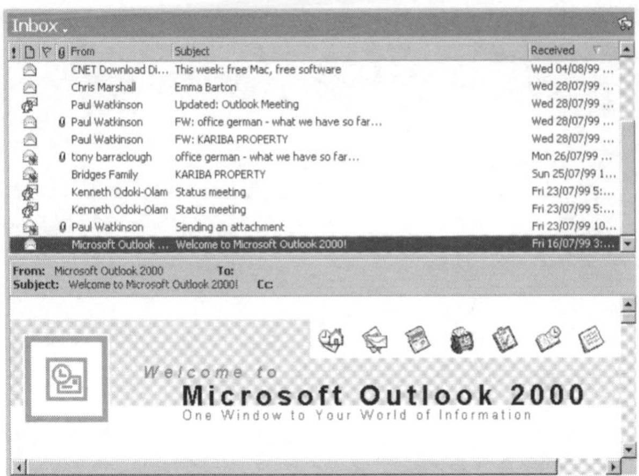

Figure 9.10 The Inbox displays your e-mail messages, both sent and received.

■ Creating contacts

In this folder, you will list all your clients, your colleagues, your prospects as well as their address, telephone number, e-mail address, and so on. When you have created your business cards records, you can consult this record whenever you want for your e-mail or to telephone one of your contacts directly using this folder (if you have a modem).

To create a business card, click on the **New** button in the toolbar (see Figure 9.11). Click on the **Contact** button, type title, name and surname of the relevant person, then click on **OK**. Type in all the other required options. Once you have finished, click on the **Save and New** button to save your business card and open a new blank card, or click on the **Save and Close** button if you do not wish to enter another business card.

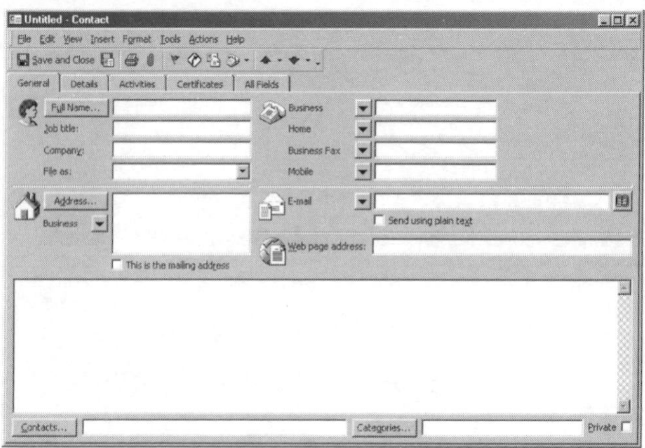

Figure 9.11 Creating a business card in the Contacts dialog.

Once you have entered your business cards, they will appear in the Contacts folder, in alphabetical order. When you require access to one of them, click on the first letter of the contact name in the **Alphabet** tab.

To select a business card, click on it. To display all the information it contains, double-click on the card.

Making a telephone call from a business card

You will be able to change your computer into a programmable telephone thanks to Outlook but only if you have a modem connected to your computer and to your telephone line, and on condition that your telephone is connected to your modem.

To make a telephone call, click on the business card of the person you wish to call, then the **Dial** button in the Standard toolbar. Click on the number you wish to call. The **New Call** dialog box is displayed(see Figure 9.12). Click on the **Start**

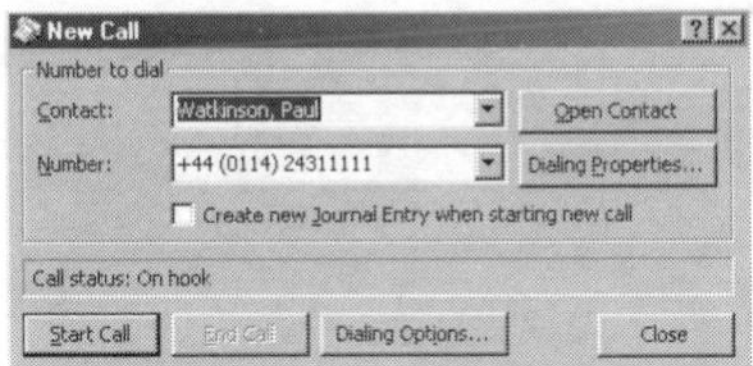

Figure 9.12 Telephoning a client or prospective client through Outlook.

Call button. Outlook dials your correspondent's number and displays a dialog box which prompts you to lift the receiver. Click on the **Speak** button when you get through to your correspondent. Click on **End Call** when the conversation is over.

Sending e-mail messages to your contacts

If your contact has an e-mail address, you can send a message from the Contacts folder.

To send an e-mail message, click on the person's business card, then on the **New Call** button in the Standard toolbar. A dialog box is displayed which contains the address of the contact you have selected. Type a title in the **Object** text box, type the complete message in the large message area positioned in the bottom part of the dialog box, then click on the **Send** button.

■ Managing tasks

To create a task, click on the Tasks folder icon in the Outlook bar. Click on the **New** button in the Standard toolbar. Click on the **Task** tab to display it, if it is not already displayed (see Figure 9.13). In the **Subject** box, type the subject or the definition of your task. In the **Due date** box, click on the **None** check box if you do not wish to set an end date for your task, or else choose the date you wish to set as the end

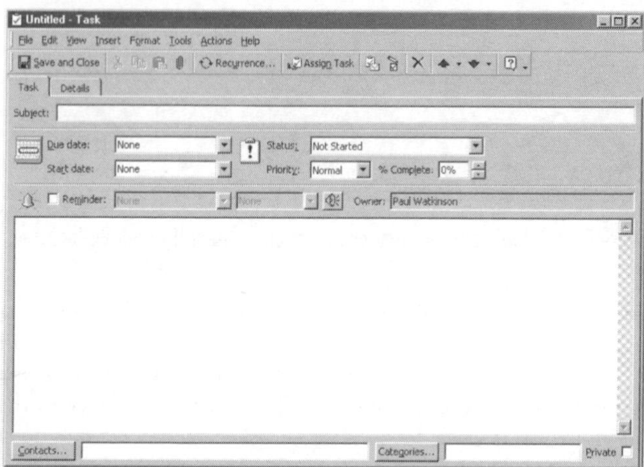

Figure 9.13 Creating a task, using various fields and options.

date in the same box, either by entering a date or by clicking on the appropriate date in the pop-down calendar. State, if necessary, the start date in the **Start date** box. The **Status** option allows you to assign a holiday period during the implementation of the task. You can also indicate a priority level, a completion percentage, a reminder signal – with sound, if you want – defined by date and time, a category, and so on. Once you have defined your choices, click on the **Save and Close** button. The task you have created is displayed in the tasks list in the Tasks folder as well as in Calendar.

When a task is completed, click on the check box in front of the completed task in the tasks list. A tick appears in the check box and Outlook crosses it to indicate that it is complete. If you wish to delete it, select it, then click on the **Delete** button in the Standard toolbar.

10 Advanced Outlook functions

Using Calendar

Sending and receiving e-mail messages

In this chapter, we will study the advanced functions of Outlook, such as creating appointments, organising meetings, sending messages, and so on.

Using Calendar

Outlook puts a Calendar at your disposal to record your appointments, plan your meetings, organise your planning and your holidays. You can also use this function to remind you about a meeting in good time for you to get ready for it.

Before we look at the procedures you need to follow in order to record and plan your time, you should get to know the terminology used in Outlook:

- An *appointment* impacts on your working time but affects only your personal time.
- A *meeting* impacts on your working time but it also affects the time of people participating in the meeting.
- An *event* is an activity spanning a whole day but not affecting your own time. A yearly event is periodical.

Customise your working week on the basis of your various activities. For example, you never work on a Wednesday to enable you to look after your little angels, or you play golf every Friday afternoon. Obviously, you are well aware of these portions of free time and you do not need reminding. But, if you are setting up a network and one of your colleagues wants to call a meeting, he is not to know that on Fridays, at 4 pm, you always play golf!

To customise your working week:

1. Click on **Tools, Options**.
2. Click on the **Calendar Options** button. Define your choices – work day, first day of week, start and end time, and so on (see Figure 10.1).

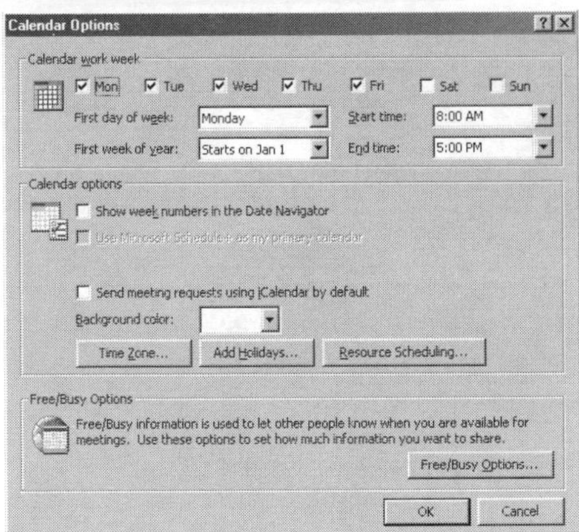

Figure 10.1 Customising your working week with the Calendar Options dialog.

Views

Outlook allows you to modify the Calendar view: click on **View**, **Current View**. In the submenu, select a view.

By default, a single day is displayed in Calendar. If you wish to modify this setting, click on one of the proposed buttons in the toolbar – Day, Work Week, and so on (see Figure 10.2).

Recording an appointment

To record an appointment, you have a choice of two procedures, one which is quick and simple, the other slightly longer but more accurate.

To create an appointment quickly, click on the date you want on the dates panel. The selected date is displayed in the work time. Click on the required time box. Type a brief description of your appointments, then press the **Enter** key to confirm.

To create a more detailed appointment, click on the **New** button in the Standard toolbar. The Untitled – Appointment

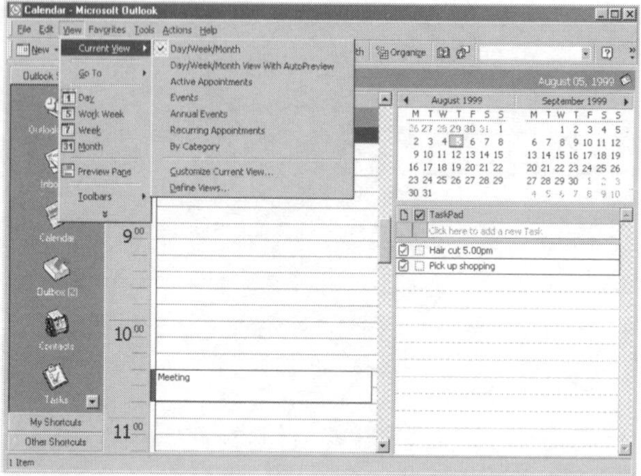

Figure 10.2 The main types of View.

dialog box is displayed (see Figure 10.3). If necessary, click on the **Appointment** tab. Specify the following options:

- **Subject.** Allows you to enter a description for the appointment.
- **Location.** Allows you to specify the appointment address.
- **Start time.** Opens a pop-down list of dates and times. If the appointment is likely to last for the whole day, tick the **All day event** check box to activate it.
- **End time.** Opens a pop-down list which allows you to specify the estimated end date and time for the appointments.
- **Reminder.** Allows you to activate or to deactivate a sound signal and to specify how long before the appointment you wish to be reminded.
- **Attendee Availability.** Allows you to specify the status of a time block. For example, when you are on a training

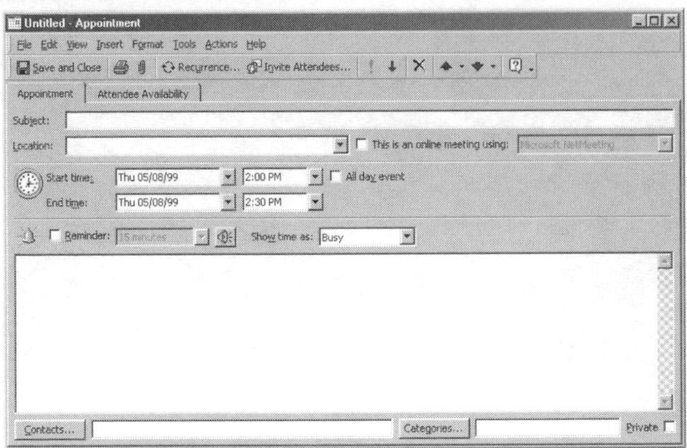

Figure 10.3 The Appointment dialog box.

course, you will mark such a day with the 'Out of Office' option.

- **Text box.** Allows you to enter additional information concerning the appointment.

Once you have finished specifying options, click on the **Save and Close** button: your appointment is displayed in your work time window (see Figure 10.4). According to the options you have chosen, a number of symbols are displayed, which will allow you to see the appointments options at a glance.

To move an appointment within the same day, click on its time box, with the mouse button pressed, then drag into the new time box.

To delete an appointment, click with the right mouse button on the appointment time box, then select **Clear**.

To prolong or reduce the length of an appointment, drag the upper or lower border of the appointment time box.

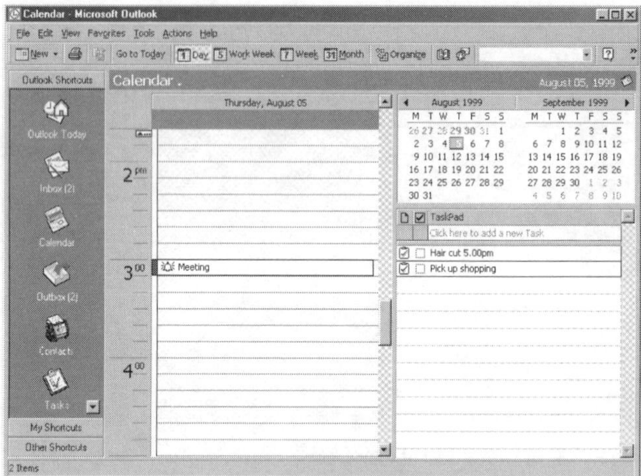

Figure 10.4 The new appointment is displayed.

Regular appointments

When an appointment is a regular occurrence on a monthly or yearly basis (for example the regular Friday marketing meeting), Outlook allows you to enter the appointment once only, specifying that it is regular. Therefore you will not need to enter your appointment for every single Friday.

To create a regular appointment:

1. Double-click on the regular appointment time box or click on the **New** button. Click on the **Recurrence** button in the dialog box toolbar (see Figure 10.5).
2. Specify the recurrence pattern, the duration, the range of recurrence, and so on. Click on **OK** to confirm your choice in the Recurrence dialog box. Click on the **Save and Close** button in the appointment dialog box.

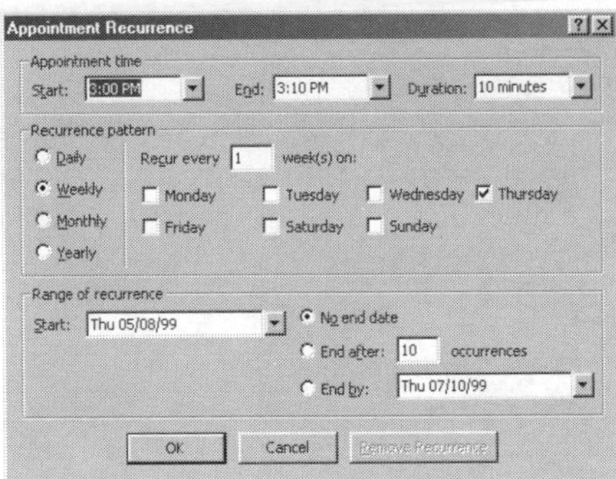

Figure 10.5 The Appointment Recurrence dialog box.

Planning a meeting

With Outlook, when you are planning your next business meeting, you no longer need all those unending telephone calls to your various colleagues to find out which day they are available. Outlook puts the Appointment Manager at your disposal, which allows you to specify the time range which is likely to suit everybody. However, this can work only if all your colleagues also use Outlook, and their work time schedule is correct and up to date.

To organise a meeting:

1. Click on **New, New Appointment.** Provide all the specifications for the meeting (date, time, and so on). Click on the **Attendee Availability** tab, then on the **Invite others** button. The **Select Attendees and Resources** dialog box is displayed: this lists the various contacts created in the address book (see Figure 10.6).
2. If required, click on the arrow of the **Name** pop-down list, then click on the address book you wish to use to choose the names of the participants: **Contacts, Outlook Address**

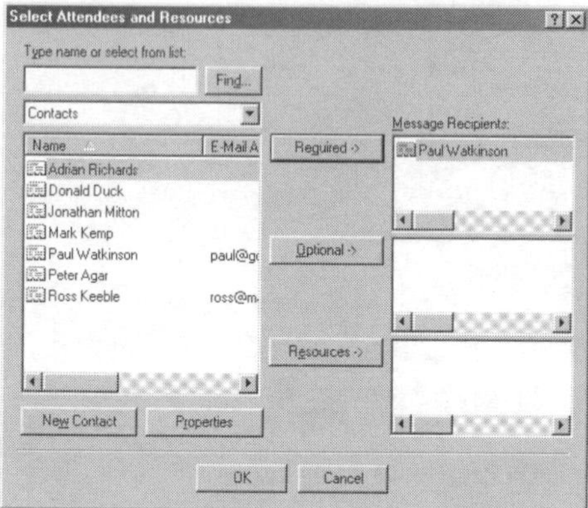

Figure 10.6 Selecting participants in the Attendees and Resources dialog.

book or **Personal Address book.** To invite somebody to the meeting, click on their name in the list, then on one of the buttons on the right (**Required, Optional** and **Resources**). Click on **OK** when all the participants have been included.

3. To check the availability of each participant, click on their name, then use the scroll bar, in the planning area, to select a time when everybody is available. Alternatively, click on the **AutoPick** button to show the next available time block suitable to all participants. When you have found a time that suits everybody, drag the vertical bars which mark the start and the end of the meeting. Click with the right mouse button on the icon in front of each participant and select **Send meeting to this attendee.** Click on **Send** and close the dialog box.

Outlook sends the convocation to all invited people. Their replies will arrive in your folder Inbox.

Recording an event

Events allows you to remember important dates and avoid painful memory lapses. You will no longer have to put up with your wife's (or your husband's) long face when you forget your wedding anniversary: thanks to Outlook, this will never happen again. But only if you have put the event down in your diary, obviously.

To record an event, click on **Actions, New All Day event** (see Figure 10.8). Specify the event subject. Type the event place in the **Location** option. Click on the arrow of the **Start time**

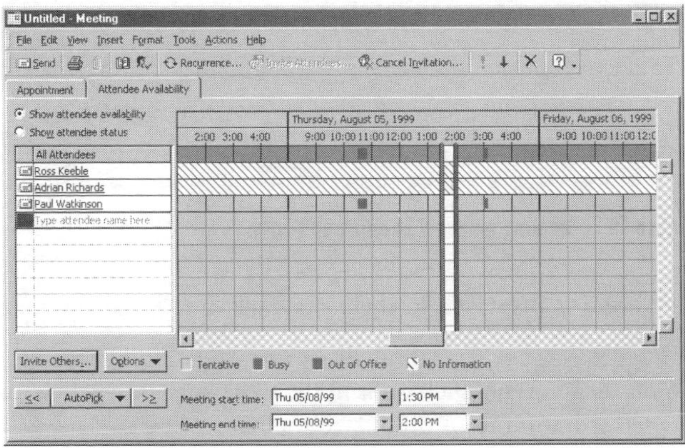

Figure 10.7 Verifying the availability of participants in your meeting.

option, then select a date. Click on the arrow of the **End time** option, then select the date. If necessary, tick the **All day event** option. If you want to, tick the **Reminder** check box, then click on the arrow and select how long before the event you wish Outlook to send out the sound signal. If you want to, specify your availability, put down some comments and select a category. Once you have finished, click on the **Save and Close** button.

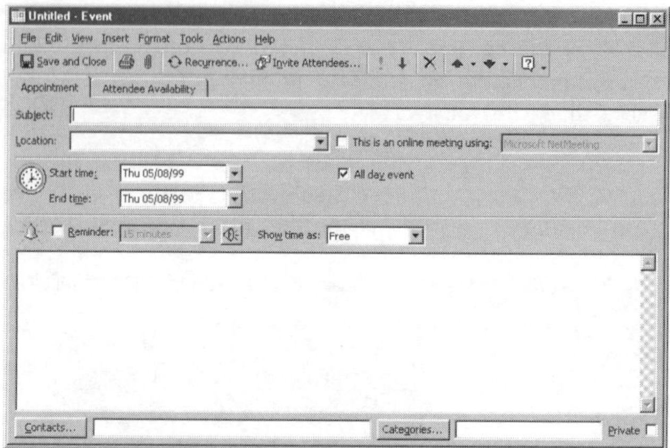

Figure 10.8 Creating an event is quick and easy.

The event is displayed in the work time of the relevant day, greyed.

To delete an event, click on it in the work time, then click on the **Clear** button in the Standard toolbar.

*To modify an event, double-click on the event in the work time. Carry out your modifications in the dialog box which is displayed, then click on the **Save and Close** button.*

■ Sending and receiving e-mail messages

When you start Outlook for the first time, the Inbox contains a single message, from Microsoft, which welcomes you. Afterwards, all messages will be displayed in this folder. The Inbox folder is displayed by default when you start Outlook.

To have better control of your messages, check the markers displayed as column headers, at the top of the receive area (see Figure 10.9):

- **Importance.** The presence of this icon indicates that the sender has given the message priority.
- **Icon.** Shows a sealed envelope. When you double-click on a message to read it, the envelope opens.
- **Flag Status.** Displays a flag if you have chosen to mark the message to read it again later or to reply to it.
- **Attachment.** Specifies that the sender has attached a file to the message. You can either view the attached file, or you can save it on your hard disk.
- **From.** Displays the sender's name.
- **Subject.** Displays a brief description of the contents of the message.
- **Received.** Displays the date and time the message was received.

To read a message, double-click on it in the list.

To sort messages according to their subject or their importance, click on the header corresponding to the marker you

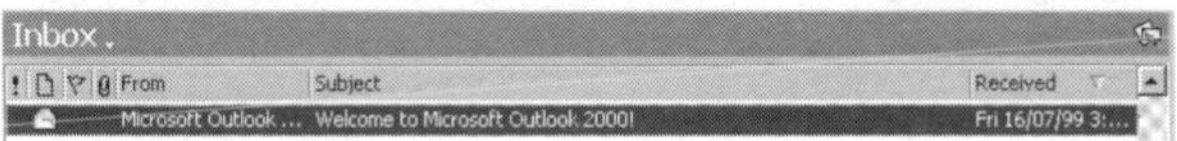

Figure 10.9 The Inbox displays all the e-mail messages you have received.

wish to use to sort your messages. For example, if you wish to sort your messages by importance, click on **Importance**.

If you wish the markers to be displayed in a different order, click on the header to be moved, then drag it to where you want it to be. To delete one of the headers, click on it, then drag it outside the bar.

The **My Shortcuts** button, at the bottom of the Outlook bar, offers other e-mail folders. This group allows you to sort sent messages, messages to be sent later and deleted items.

E-mail configuration

For Outlook to display your mail, it must know with which e-mail service you are working.

Once you have installed the directory service program, add it to the list of services that Outlook can use:

1. Click on **Tools**, **Accounts**: the directory services that Outlook can currently use are listed.
2. Click on the **Add** button, then on the name of the service in the list, and then on **OK**.
3. The Wizard may ask for additional information depending on the directory service you wish to install. For example, it may ask for your name and your fax number, or to select the fax/modem you are going to use. When you have finished, click on **OK**.

Now, you can use Outlook to manage your messages.

Sending messages

To create a message, click on the **New** button in the Standard toolbar (see Figure 10.10). In the **To** text box, type the e-mail address of the person to whom you are sending the message. If you have it stored in the Contacts folder, you do not need to type it all over again. Simply click on the **To** button, then select the name of the person from the list in the dialog box which is displayed. If you wish to send a copy of this message to another person, click on the **Cc** button, then select the person to whom you wish to send the copy in the list or type their URL (e-mail address) in the text box. When you must enter several addresses, separate them with a colon (:).

Once you have filled the addressee boxes, you must absolutely fill the **Subject** box. Then, in the bottom part of the window, type your message. If you are sending only text, click on the **Send** button. But if you wish to attach a file to your

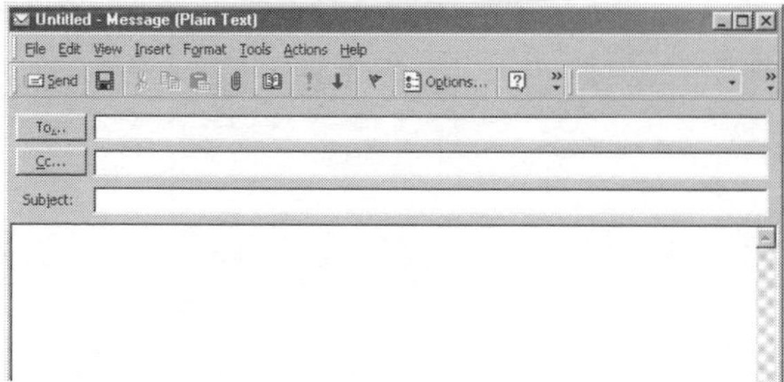

Figure 10.10 Entering your e-mail message.

message or indicate an option in terms of importance, choose one of the following procedures:

- To format the text, drag your pointer on to the relevant text, then choose font, size and attributes in the toolbar.
- To attach a file to your message, click on the **Insert File** button, then select the file you wish to attach in the displayed dialog box.
- To flag the message, click on the **Flag for Follow Up** button. In the dialog box which is displayed, specify the options (**Flag to**, **Clear Flag**, **Due by**, and so on).
- To indicate the degree of importance for the message, click on the **Importance: High** or **Importance: Low** buttons.
- The **Options** button offers other choices to create buttons for tracking, accepting, refusing, and so on (see Figure 10.11).

Receiving messages

When you are working in Outlook and you want to know whether you have any new messages, click on **Tools**, **Check New Mail** or press the **F5** key. Outlook then connects to the installed server, retrieves your messages, then displays them in your Inbox list.

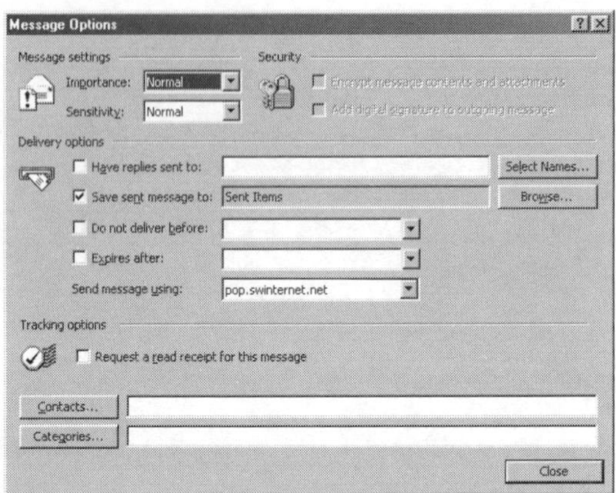

Figure 10.11 E-mail message options.

To read your message, double-click on it. Outlook displays the message in the window. This window offers various buttons:

- **Reply.** Allows you to send a reply message to the sender. Click on this button to open a message window with the sender's address (the person who has sent you the original message to which you are now replying). The text of the original message is also displayed in the text box. You can clear it or keep it. Type your reply, then click on the **Send** button.
- **Reply All.** Allows you to send a reply to all the people on the **To** or **Cc** lists.
- **Transfer.** Allows you to send the message directly to another person.
- **Back** or **Next.** Allows you to scroll through all your messages.

11 Basic Publisher functions

In this chapter, we will study the basic functions of Publisher such as frames, views, text insertion, and so on.

Discovering Publisher

To start Publisher, click on **Start**, **Programs**, **Microsoft Publisher**.

The Catalog dialog box

When Publisher starts, the Catalog dialog box is displayed (see Figure 11.1): this allows you to choose a Wizard, to open an existing publication or even to choose a style. You need to know that:

- The **Publications by Wizard** tab allows you to use a Wizard which will guide you throughout the creation process.

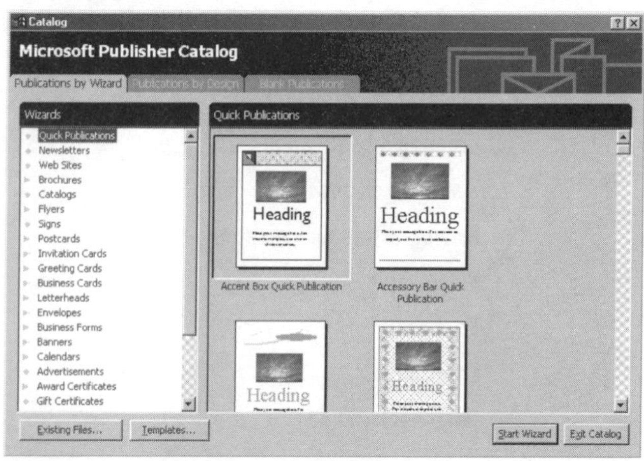

Figure 11.1 The Catalog dialog box allows you to choose a Wizard, to open an existing publication or to choose a style.

- The **Publications by Design** tab allows you to preview different publications created with a variety of designs such as geometrical shapes, a series of pictures, and so on.
- The **Blank Publications** tab allows you to choose a preset type of publication according to its actual use (Web page, Postcard, and so on).
- The **Existing Files** button allows you to open an already created publication.
- The **Templates** button allows you to select an Office template to create the publication.

To display the Catalog dialog box, click on ***File, New****.*

To open an existing publication in the Catalog dialog box, click on the **Existing Files** button (see Figure 11.2), then double-click on the publication to be opened.

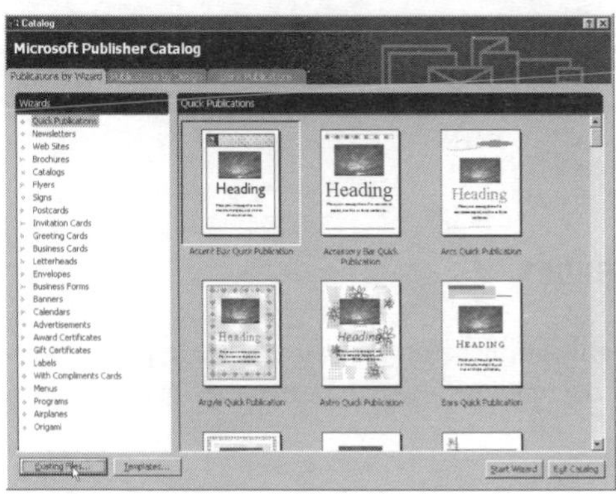

Figure 11.2 Opening an existing file.

Publication with assistance

To facilitate the process, Publisher offers a number of possibilities to create a publication quickly. These tools are called Wizards and templates or styles (see Chapter 1).

Use Wizards or templates when you need to create an effective, attractive and well-structured publication in a very short time.

■ Creating a publication

As already stated, the Catalog dialog box is the central point for managing publications. It is therefore from here that you can open a blank publication:

1. In the Catalog dialog box, click on the **Blank Publications** tab (see Figure 11.3). Click on the category in the left pane, then on the type in the right pane.
2. Click on the **Create** button.

To choose a new publication, you can either click on its textual description in the left pane or on its graphic description in the right pane.

■ Managing pages

By default, a blank publication contains a single page, in the chosen format. You can add, delete, move or copy pages in a publication.

Inserting pages

A publication rarely has only a single page; this is how you insert pages:

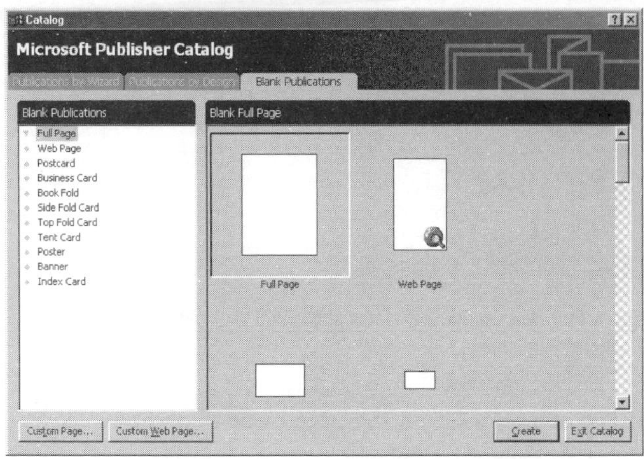

Figure 11.3 Choosing the style of a new publication in the Blank Publications tab of the Catalog dialog.

1. Click on **Insert**, **Page** (see Figure 11.4).
2. Specify the number of pages you require to insert in the **Number of new pages** box. Then, specify where you wish to insert the new pages (before or after the existing page). Click on **OK**.

   The new publication is displayed, with page numbers, in the Status bar.

Deleting pages

To delete a blank page, simply click on **Edit, Delete Page.** Confirm the deletion by clicking on OK.

Copying a page

If you wish to create several similar pages, it is simpler just to copy your page:

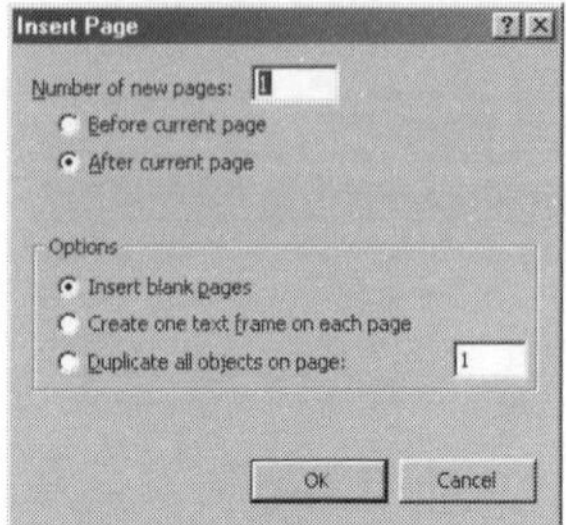

Figure 11.4 You can quickly insert pages into your publication with the Insert Page dialog.

1. Position yourself on the page to be duplicated. Click on **Insert, Page.**
2. Select the **Duplicate all objects on page** option. Specify the number of copies you require in the **Number of new pages** box. Specify whether you wish to insert them, then click on **OK**.

■ Moving within a publication

The simpler and faster method is to use the Status bar (see Figure 11.5). In this bar, the number of the active page on the screen is displayed in the Page box. To move between pages, click on the symbol of the page to be displayed.

To move in the page, use the scroll bar: drag the bar in the direction you wish to move.

■ Views

There are many View options in Publisher. The Page view corresponds to the way you will view the page on screen and,

Figure 11.5 The Status bar allows you to move quickly from one page to another.

eventually, display certain special characters. The default page view in a publication is a single page, with a 33% zoom.

When you create a publication which contains several pages, you can choose to display two pages next to each other. Click on **View**, **Two-Page Spread** (see Figure 11.6). To navigate between two pages in the double-page spread, simply click on the page in which you wish to work. To go back to single-page view, click on **View**, **Two-Page Spread** to deactivate it.

33% To modify the size of a page view, click on the arrow in the Zoom pop-down list and select the display view. You can also click on **View**, **Zoom**.

*The **Whole Page** option in the Zoom command displays the whole of the page on screen, with a 33% zoom.*

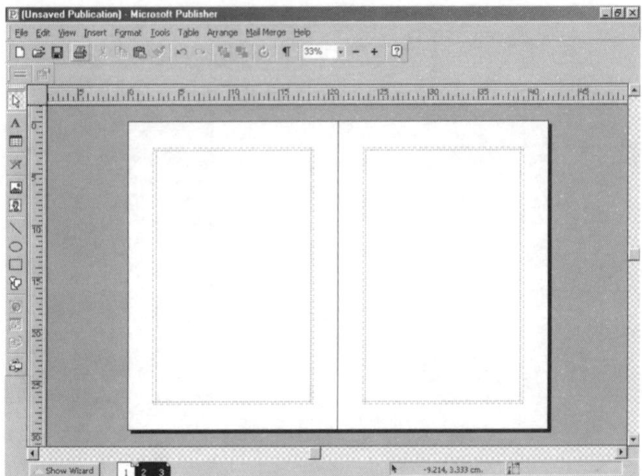

Figure 11.6 You can also view pages as spreads.

Frames

In Publisher, any elements you want to create must be within a frame. This applies to all DTP applications even though, in some cases, this may not be so obvious. Why frames? Because this is the most practical way to manage elements such as text or a picture, and to place them in the right position, to move them, and so on. To understand this concept better, think of it like a puzzle. When you start a puzzle, you know what you need to achieve as the final outcome. Your page is this final outcome; each frame which you insert into it is therefore like a piece of the puzzle.

Inserting a frame

Each element is inserted from a task-specific frame (text frame, image, and so on). To insert a frame:

1. Click on the **Frame Tool...** icon on the Objects toolbar.
2. Click on the page, then drag diagonally to be able to draw a frame (see Figure 11.7).

To do it even faster, having selected Frame Tool, double-click anywhere on the page: the frame is automatically inserted.

*If, when you click on the page, you do not create a text frame, click on **Tools, Options**. In the **Edit** tab, click on the **Use single-click object creation** option. Click on **OK**.*

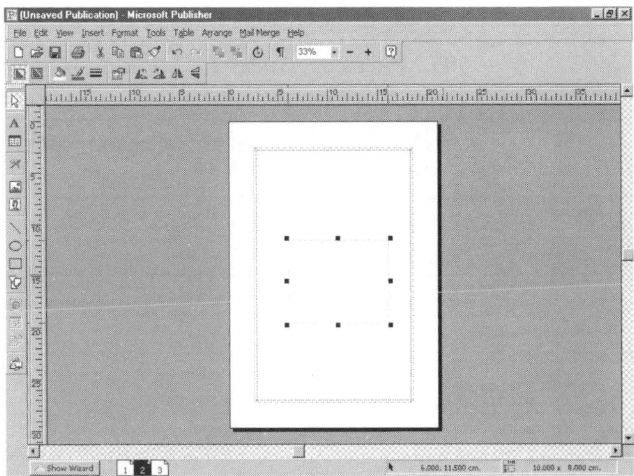

Figure 11.7 Inserting a text frame.

Selecting and working on a frame

To be able to work on the text frames you have inserted, you must select them. To select a frame, simply click on it. The frame becomes surrounded by small black squares, known as *selection handles*. To resize the object, position the mouse pointer over a selection handle and drag. To move the object, drag the border between two selection handles.

According to the handle you are using, you will see an icon with a textual description which indicates the action you can execute. Refer to Table 11.1 to get to know the use for each pointer.

Table 11.1 Description of pointer symbols

Pointer	Action
MOVE	Moves the selection.
RESIZE	Widens or reduces the selection to the right.
RESIZE	Widens or reduces the selection from the right to the left.
RESIZE	Widens or reduces the selection from top to bottom.
RESIZE	Widens or reduces the selection from the left to the right.
CROP	Clears the selection.

To deselect a frame, simply click outside it.

To delete a frame with nothing inserted, click in the frame to select it, then press on the **Del** key.

To delete a frame which contains an element (text, image, and so on), click in the frame to select it, then click on **Edit, Delete Object**.

To resize the frame, position the mouse pointer over a selection handle and drag until you reach the required size. To move the object, drag the border between two selection handles.

To resize a frame retaining its original proportions, press the ***Shift*** *key and keep it pressed while you drag one of the corner handles. Release the Shift key when you have finished resizing the frame.*

Before moving a frame, you must select it. Point to one of the frame borders (but without putting the pointer on a selection handle). The pointer becomes a little cross and displays an icon representing a small van with Move written on it. Click on it, then drag to where you want to position the text frame.

Connecting frames

We may have misjudged the size of a text: the text to be displayed in the frame does not fit into it. You can widen the frame to make the whole text visible, or create a second frame and connect these two frames; in this way the text 'in overflow' will spill automatically into the connected frame.

To connect frames:

1. When the text in a first frame is too long, you will see the **Text in Overflow** icon (see Figure 11.8). Select the frame which is too small and click on **Tools**, **Connect Text Frames**.
2. Click on the **Connect Text Frames** button in the Standard toolbar.

   The mouse pointer changes to a pitcher.
3. Click in the text frame in which you want your story to continue (see Figure 11.9). The text from your story now 'flows' into the second frame.

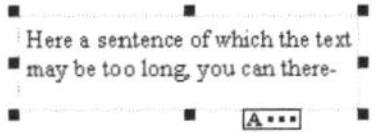

Figure 11.8 Text surrounded by the frame.

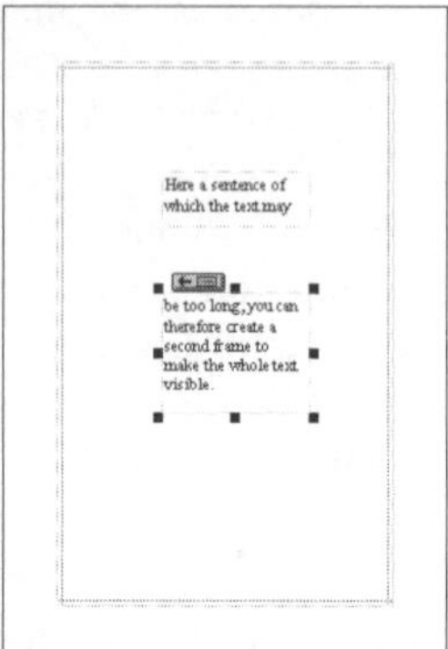

Figure 11.9 Linking text frames allows the text to flow from one frame to another.

To disconnect two connected frames, click on the first frame of the connection, then on the ***Disconnect Text Frames*** *icon in the Standard toolbar.*

Entering text

To enter text, you must first select the frame which will contain it. The selection activates a flashing cursor which shows the insertion point for your text. Then type your text.

All text editing, moving and copying functions are exactly as in Word. Refer to Chapter 3.

Importing text

You can also insert into a frame text which has been saved in another application. Publisher can import several text file types such as Microsoft Windows Word (2.1, 6.0, 7.0 and 8.0), text only, RTF, and so on.

To import text into your publication:

1. Create the text frame, then click on **Insert, Text File.**
2. Select the type of text to be inserted in the **Files of type** box, then display the folder which contains the file you want. Double-click on the file and insert.

Text formatting

Character formatting can be done either before or after entry:

- **Before entry.** Select attributes, styles and options required, then type your text.
- **After entry.** Select the text to be formatted, then choose attributes, styles and options to be applied.

Formatting tools

Publisher offers two tools to format characters: the Format toolbar and the Font formatting command. These tools are exactly the same as the ones used in Word (see Chapter 3). Here we will look at formatting which is specific to Publisher.

Scaling corresponds to spacing characters within the same word. In the past, this word was used to describe the mark on the metal cast of a character.

To modify scaling for a word or a text:

1. Click on **Format, Character Spacing** (see Figure 11.10).
2. The Tracking area allows you to adjust the spacing for a highlighted block of text. The Kerning area allows you to fine-tune the spacing between two characters (Expand, Condense or Normal). Define the formatting to be applied. Click on **OK**.

You can create an interesting visual effect by rotating text. Once you have selected your text, use the **Rotation left** icon to rotate it by 45° to the left, the **Rotation right** icon to rotate it by 45° to the right.

Figure 11.10 Defining the tracking and kerning of text.

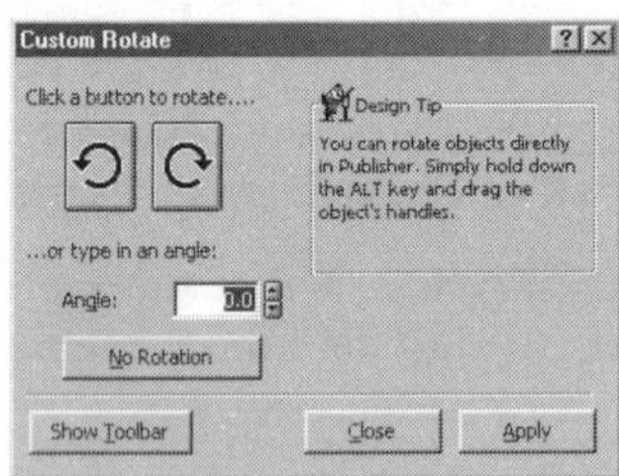

Figure 11.11 Rotating your text.

To execute a precise rotation:

1. Select the text, then click on the **Custom Rotate** icon in the Standard toolbar (see Figure 11.11).
2. Click on the button which offers the orientation to be applied (left or right), which allows you to rotate 5° with each click, or type the required rotation value in the **Angle** box. Click on **Apply**, then on **Close**.

■ Page background

To understand the background concept, imagine that each page in your publication has two layers: the first layer – the first level – contains the items which make up the page (text frames, image frames, objects, and so on); the second layer – the background – contains all the items required for the whole of the publication (page number, headers, footers, fill colour, and so on).

To display the background of a page, click on **View, Go to Background**: the page you have been working on which displayed all you had created so far becomes blank, the Status bar changes and the pages navigator disappears.

The background allows you to position:

- a rule, a frame or a line;
- a name, a reference or a logo;
- a drawing as a watermark;
- a pagination;
- a header and a footer;
- a date.

Do not forget that all the insertions executed in the background, whatever they may be, will appear on all the pages in the active publication. However, you may choose to exclude some of the pages from showing the background items.

*To avoid displaying the defined background in one of the publication pages, go to the relevant page and click on **View, Ignore Background.***

The first thing you can achieve with the background is the creation of a background colour for your publication pages.

To display a coloured background:

1. Click on **Text Frame Tool** in the Object toolbar. Draw a frame all around your page.
2. Once you have selected the background, click on the **Fill Color** icon in the Format toolbar. Select the required colour.

Page numbering, header, footer and date

If you create a publication which has only a single page, you will not need to bother with page numbering. However, publications usually contain several pages, so you will need to know how to paginate them. In order to insert a number of pages, you must create a text frame in the background.

To create a text frame in the background, and after having activated it, click on **Text Frame Tool**, then insert the frame into the background. Most of the time, the page number is placed at the bottom of the background, either to the right, to the left or in the middle.

*When you insert items into the background, apply **Fill Color** if your background is in colour, otherwise the inserted frame will look empty and will not be displayed in your publication.*

To insert page numbers in a document, click on the text frame which will contain the numbers, then on **Insert, Page Numbers**. This command inserts only the numbers, but you can enter *Page* before it (see Figure 11.12).

*To delete page numbers in the background, click on the frame to select it, then press on the **Del** key.*

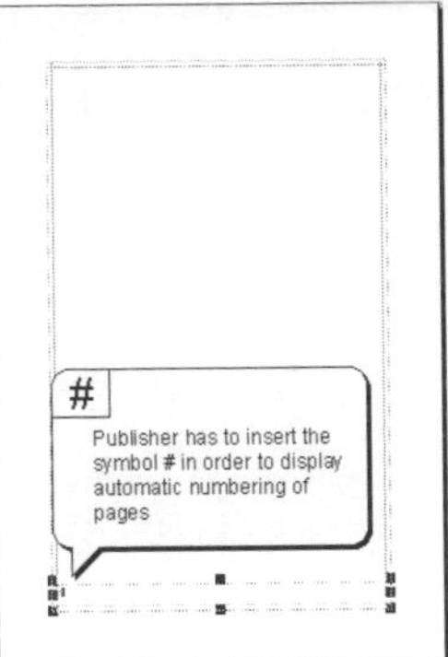

Figure 11.12 Inserting page numbers into your publication.

Inserting a header and a footer into the background is extremely easy. It is as simple as inserting a text frame into a page.

To create a footer, follow the same procedures as for a header. The difference is that you place the text frame at the bottom of the background.

To create a header in a background:

1. Create a text frame at the top of the background.
2. Type your text.
3. Apply the various formats (colour, size, font, and so on).

To delete a header in the background, click on the frame to select it, then press on the ***Del*** *key. Follow the same procedure to delete a footer.*

It is often important to be able to insert a date into a publication. For instance, you will immediately be able to tell when it was created and what modifications need to be carried out on the basis of the age of the document and the changes which may have occurred since its creation.

To insert a date into a background:

1. Create a text frame at the top or bottom of the background.
2. Click on **Insert, Date and Time.**
3. Select the format in the list.
4. Click on **OK.**

   The system date is inserted into your publication.

*To delete a date in the background, click on the frame to select it, then press the **Del** key.*

12 Advanced Publisher functions

Tables

Text in columns

Mailshots

Pictures

Picture and text

Design gallery

Drawing

Formatting objects

Managing shapes and frames

In this chapter, we will look at advanced Publisher functions such as insertion of tables, creating text in columns, mail-shots, and so on.

Tables

A table allows you to set a defined structure for data. Information becomes much clearer when data is properly presented. In Publisher, the use of tables allows better control when positioning items on the page. The basic building block for a table is the *cell*. A cell is a grid unit which may contain any type of data: text, image, and so on.

Tables have a number of properties which can be defined, such as number of rows and columns, border thickness and colour, background colour or texture, and so on.

Creating a table

Publisher allows you to create a table with no pre-defined format.

To create a table with no predefined format:

1. Click on the **Table Frame Tool** icon in the Objects toolbar. Click on the page you are working on, then drag so you can draw a table.

   The Create Table dialog box is displayed (see Figure 12.1).
2. Specify the options (number of rows, number of columns, and so on), then click on **OK**.

The default choice proposed in the Table format list corresponds to a predefined format and not to a blank table.

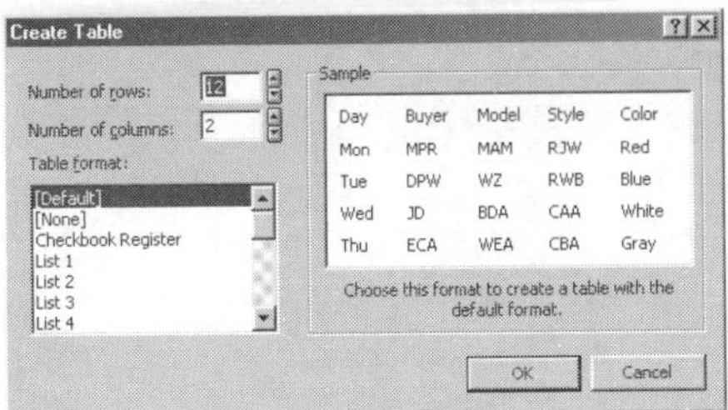

Figure 12.1 The Create Table dialog is displayed: you must now decide on the number of columns and rows.

*To delete a table: after having selected it, click on **Edit, Delete Object**.*

To enter text into a table or navigate within it, refer to the procedures shown in Word (see Chapters 3 and 4).

■ Text in columns

Obviously, you can create text frames which contain text and distribute them into columns using tabulations. However, this procedure is somewhat risky, because when you need to insert new text or even only edit it, tabulations will move and this will spell disaster! The easiest and fastest way is to create columns.

To create columns, after having created your text frame, click on **Format, Text Frame Properties** (see Figure 12.2). In the Columns area, specify the number of columns and the spacing between columns. Click on **OK**.

To modify the column, use the **Tab** key.

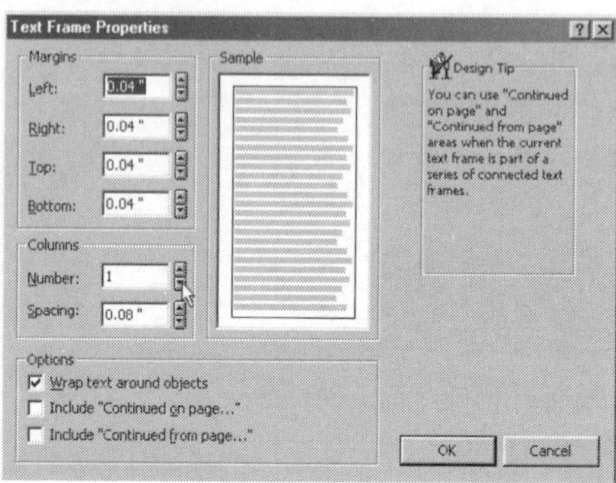

Figure 12.2 Define the number of columns.

■ Mailshots

When you execute a mail merge, you must create two types of documents:

- **Main document.** A general frame which contains text or the custom publication. This text is common to all addressees, but with reserved places for custom formulas such as address, name, and so on.
- **Database.** Contains all the personal data for your addressees. This document is also known as *data source*. It is like a table.

Once these two elements have been created, you can start printing and merging the publication. The merge consists of linking these documents by inserting the database fields into the main document, for each addressee. The various procedures to execute a mail merge are the same as in Word. See Chapter 4.

Pictures

There are several methods for inserting a picture in a publication (vector image, bmp image, card, chart, and so on). Just as for text, you must first insert a frame. The picture frame concept is the same as for the text frame: a picture frame is a separate and independent program.

ClipArt

The first of the possibilities proposed by Publisher is to insert a picture from ClipArt, the picture library put at your disposal. This library is much more exhaustive in the 2000 version, having acquired hundreds of additional pictures. Following the same principle as a book library, pictures are arranged by category. Simply choose the picture you wish to insert into your publication.

Placed in the Object toolbar, it allows you to insert a ClipArt picture. Follow the standard procedures for inserting a frame, select the picture, then drag it into the frame.

Other pictures

Publisher offers other tools to insert pictures.

To insert a picture that you have saved in one of your files:

1. After inserting a picture frame, click on **Insert**, **Pictures**, **From File**.
2. In the Insert Picture dialog box, select the folder you require. Double-click on the file which contains the picture.

Selecting and deleting pictures

To select a picture, simply click on it.

To select several pictures, select the first one, press the **Ctrl** key, then click on the second picture while keeping the key depressed, and so on. This command also allows you to move or copy the set of pictures easily.

To delete a picture, the simplest procedure is to select it, then press the **Del** key. You can also right-click on the picture, then select **Delete Object**.

Moving and copying pictures

To move a picture within the same page, the procedure is the same as for a text frame:

1. Click on the picture to select it.
2. Point to the picture frame.
3. When the pointer changes to a cross with a little van, drag to where you wish to place it.

If you wish to move a picture to another page in the publication, select it, then drag it to the greyed part, outside the page. Display the page in which you wish to insert the picture. The picture is still in the greyed part; simply place it in the new page.

To copy-paste a picture:

1. Select it, then click on **Edit, Copy**.
2. Position yourself where you require the picture to be copied.
3. Click on **Edit, Paste**.

Editing pictures

All the options for editing pictures are the same as in PowerPoint (see Chapter 7). You will find here the editing procedures which are specific to Publisher.

To hide images, click on **View**, **Picture Display**. Select the **Hide pictures** option, then click on **OK** (see Figure 12.3).

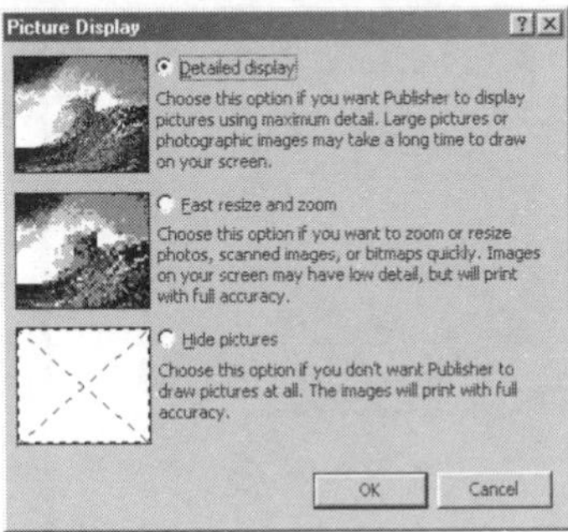

Figure 12.3 Hiding images.

To show the pictures again:

1. Click on **View, Picture Display.**
2. Select the option corresponding to your choice (**Detailed display** or **Fast resize and zoom**). Click on **OK**.

The picture is too large, but you want to keep the same proportions? Just crop a bit out:

1. After selecting the picture, click on the **Crop Picture** icon (see Figure 12.4).
2. Adjust the various selection handles until the picture shows only the items you need.

To view the picture as enlarged, click on it, then click with the right mouse button and select ***Selected Objects****.*

You can even apply a different colour to a picture according to your preference:

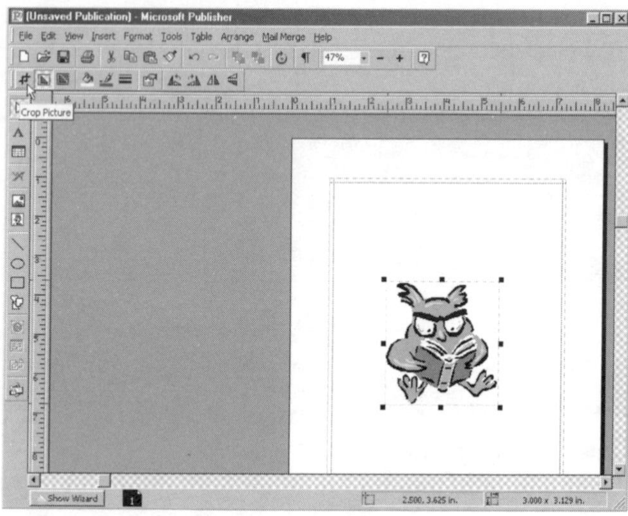

Figure 12.4 Crop the picture to suit your needs.

1. After selecting the picture, click on **Format, Color picture** (see Figure 12.5).
2. Select the required colour for the item you wish to edit.
3. Click on **Apply and Close.**

Figure 12.5 Recolor Picture.

■ Picture and text

When you create a publication, you may wish to add an amusing visual effect by inserting pictures into the text. Depending on the type of hyphenation chosen, the text will be arranged automatically around the picture. Otherwise you will have to fit the picture to the text.

To control text and picture, click on the **Picture Frame Properties** button in the Picture toolbar (see Figure 12.6). Specify your choices, then click on **OK**.

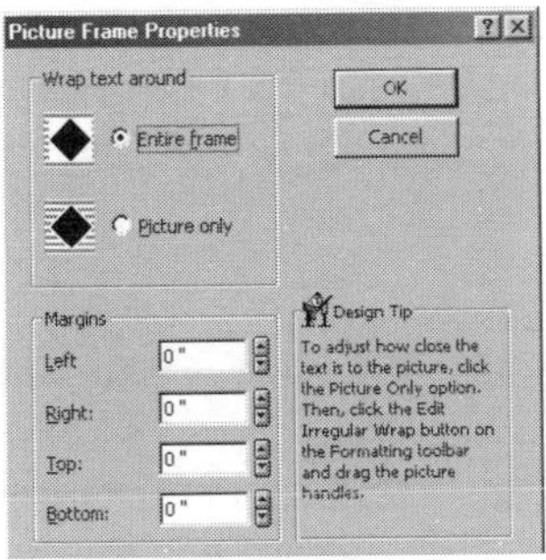

Figure 12.6 The image can be modified to affect the text.

■ Design gallery

The design gallery contains a number of objects created by Publisher which you can use for your publication. To open the design gallery, click on the **Design Gallery Object** icon in the Objects bar (see Figure 12.7).

Three tabs are proposed:

- **Objects by Category** and **Objects by Design** display a number of objects on which you simply double-click to insert them into your publication. The left pane displays a

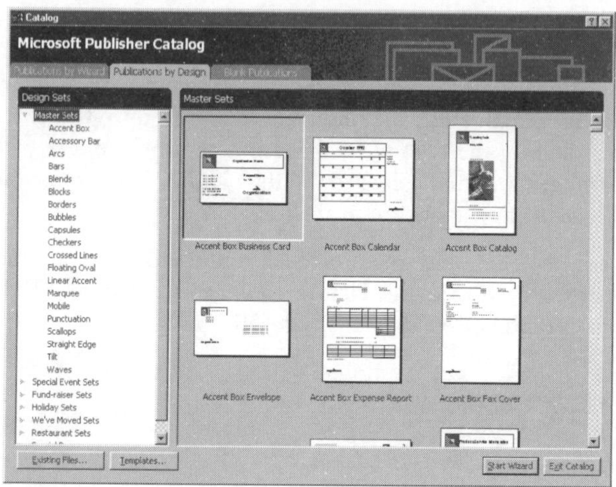

Figure 12.7 Design Gallery.

list of objects sorted by type, the right pane displays the objects of the selected type.

- **Your Objects** allows you to keep the design elements to create a set of designs for the current publication. Therefore, when you add objects, they are displayed in this tab and are then available for your publication.

■ Drawing

Publisher allows you to draw in the design page. In fact, it puts at your disposal a number of geometrical shapes which you can insert into the page, then edit at your convenience.

If you are a drawing wizard, you can also draw directly in the design page.

Inserting drawings on your page

If you feel that you are up to drawing directly in the design page, you must first choose one of the drawing programs installed on your PC.

To draw from a drawing program:

1. In the relevant design page, click on **Insert, Object.**

*In the Insert Object dialog box, the **Create from file** option allows you to find on your PC the file which will be used for creating your drawings.*

2. If necessary, click on the **Create New** option to activate it. In the pop-down list, select the program to execute your drawing. Click on **OK** to confirm (see Figure 12.8).

   The various tools of the selected program are displayed in the active publication in the frame in which you are going to create your drawing.
3. Resize the design frame as you like.
4. Create your design. When you have finished, click outside the frame to go back to the publication.

To go back to the drawing that you have created, simply double-click on the frame which contains it.

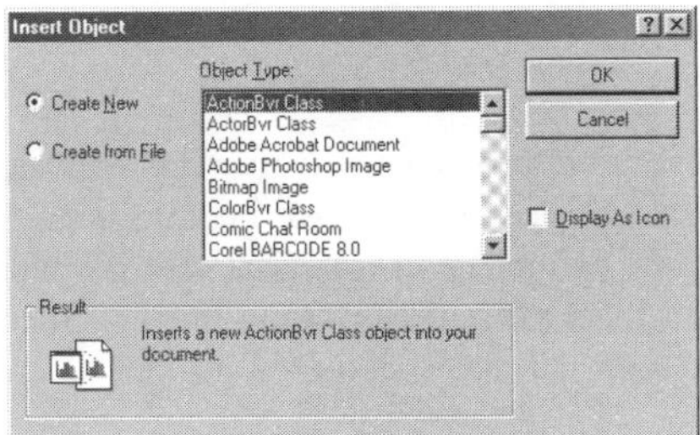

Figure 12.8 Choose one of the graphics applications installed on your PC.

Inserting shapes

As we have just seen, creating a drawing from a drawing application was up to now only for click magicians. Recognising this problem, the programmers who created Publisher have generated a number of geometrical shapes that can be inserted and formatted.

The shapes proposed in the Objects toolbar are the following:

- **Line Tool.** Allows you to trace lines.
- **Oval Tool.** Allows you to insert circles or ellipses.
- **Rectangle Tool.** Allows you to insert squares or rectangles.

*When you draw using any of these tools, always remember to click on **Tool Selector** to deselect tool when your drawing is complete.*

To insert a drawing, simply click on the relevant tool, then on the page and drag upwards to achieve the size you want.

*To draw a square, when you click on **Rectangle Tool**, press on the **Shift** key, then keep it pressed all the time while drawing the square.*

Inserting custom shapes

As well as traditional shapes, Publisher puts at your disposal a number of custom shapes from the star to the sun, including arrows, polygons and moon crescents. These shapes will give your publication a fresh and pleasing look with a touch of originality. Just as with standard shapes, you can easily format these items.

 You can select a shape from the Custom Shapes tool in the Objects toolbar.

To insert a custom shape:

1. Click on the **Custom Shapes** tool in the Objects toolbar.
2. In the menu which is displayed, click on the required shape (see Figure 12.9). Click on the drawing page, then, keeping the button pressed, drag the required shape.

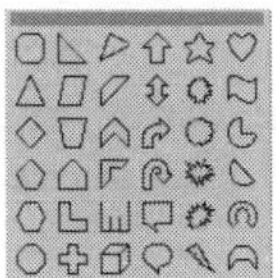

Figure 12.9 Choose the Custom Shape to be included from the menu that is displayed.

Deleting shapes

To delete a shape, click on it to select it, then press the **Del** key.

■ Formatting objects

Now that you have learned how to insert lines, squares, ellipses, and so on, let us have a look at the various formatting possibilities proposed by Publisher. First, however, we need to look at how to move and resize objects.

Selecting, resizing and moving simple objects

All standard or custom shapes, lines, and so on which you insert into your publication are perceived by Publisher as objects. As such, you can move, edit or delete them.

Selecting an object is the same as selecting a frame. Click on the relevant object: several handles will appear, which you can use to resize and move your object. The number of handles depends on the selected object: a line has two handles, a circle six.

To move an object quickly, after selecting it, point to the object, then click on it and hold down the mouse button when the pointer icon changes to a cross with a small van. Move it to where you want to be, then release the mouse button.

To move an object precisely, select it, then click on **Format, Size and Position.** In the Position area of the dialog box which is displayed, specify the exact position for your object, then click on **OK** (see Figure 12.10).

To resize an object quickly, select it, point to one of the handles, then click on it when the Size icon changes to an arrow pointing in the required direction. Drag to achieve the required size, then release the mouse button.

To resize an object exactly, select it, then click on **Format, Size and Position.** In the Size area of the dialog box which is displayed, specify the exact size for your object, then click on **OK** to confirm.

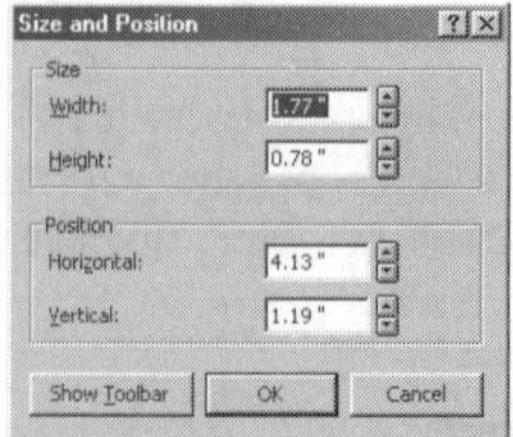

Figure 12.10 The Size and Position dialog box allows you to resize an image and place it precisely on the page.

Formatting lines

Publisher offers several options for formatting lines inserted into your publication.

To modify a line thickness, select it, then click on the **Line/Border Style** icon. In the menu which is displayed, select the required thickness (see Figure 12.11). The **More Styles** choice allows you to select or specify a precise size, the shape of the line tip, and so on.

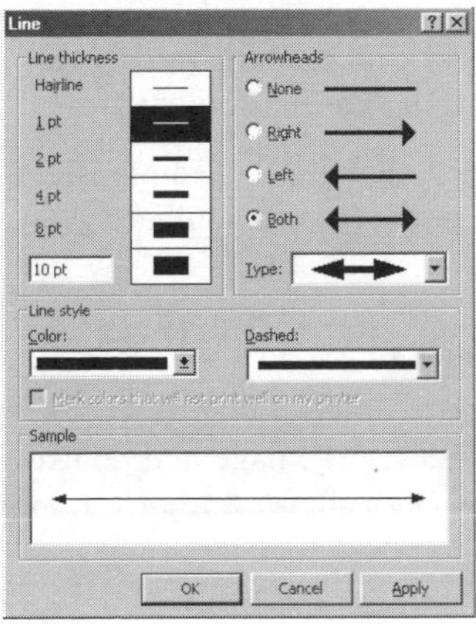

Figure 12.11 You can choose from a variety of line thicknesses and arrowheads.

To modify the tips of your line, select the line, then click on one of the arrow icons proposed in the Format toolbar.

*The **Line** dialog box allows you to choose other arrowhead options which are not in the Format toolbar.*

Formatting standard and custom shapes

Publisher allows you to modify colour, surface or even thickness for both standard and custom shapes.

To modify the outline of an object, select it, then click on the **Line/Border Style** icon in the Format toolbar. Use the same procedures as for modifying text or picture frame borders.

To modify the surface of an object, select it, then click on the **Fill Color** icon in the Format toolbar. Use the same procedure as for modifying text or picture frame colours.

Rotating and flipping objects

Publisher allows you to flip shapes and/or rotate them.

To flip an object, select it, then click on the **Flip Vertical** icon or on the **Flip Horizontal** icon in the Format toolbar.

To rotate an object, select it, then click on the **Rotate Right** icon or on the **Rotate Left** icon in the Format toolbar.

Managing shapes and frames

Publisher offers several possibilities to manage and control the various objects in your page, both shapes and picture or text frames.

Superimposing frames

When you create a publication, some frames must be superimposed. You can certainly move frames to be able to superimpose them, but how do you bring to the front the frame which is underneath?

To specify the position for a frame, select the one whose position you wish to modify. Then click on the **Bring to Front** icon or the **Send to Back** icon in the Standard toolbar.

Superimposing several objects or several frames

It is true that modifying the position of two frames or objects is relatively simple and quick, but the situation gets more complicated when you need to insert more than two objects or frames and these are stacked one on top of the other. Luckily, Publisher has thought it all out.

To modify the position of a frame or an object in a stack, select one of the objects from the top, or any of the frames or objects you can see. Click on **Arrange** and make your choice:

- **Bring to Front.** Allows you to position the selected object or frame to the front.
- **Send to Back.** Allows you to position the selected object or frame to the back.
- **Bring Backward.** Allows you to move by one stage down the selected object or frame.
- **Bring Forward.** Allows you to move by one stage up the selected object or frame.

Aligning objects

You have already tried it: creating a publication is very easy. In fact, tracing lines, creating frames or even inserting pictures can all be done very quickly. However, once you have your creations, the finishing stage is slightly harder: you need to position your items correctly, to define their alignment, and so on. For this too Publisher offers interesting possibilities.

Let us have a look at the Guides. These are horizontal or vertical lines which you place in the publication and on which you place your items to control their position.

To display Guides, click on **View, View Boundaries and Guides.**

To choose the type of guide:

1. Click on **Arrange, Ruler Guides.**
2. In the pop-down menu, select **Add Horizontal Ruler Guide** and/or **Add Vertical Ruler Guide.**

3. Click on the guide which will be shown to place it where you want (see Figure 12.12).

To delete a guide, click on ***Arrange, Ruler Guides****. In the pop-down menu, select* ***Clear All Ruler Guides****.*

You can align objects on the Guides. After having selected your frames or objects, click on **Tools, Snap to Guides.**

Figure 12.12 Show Ruler Guides to help you place objects.

Index

Common functions

F

G

H

I

M

N

O

W

Excel

A

B

C

Outlook

A

C

D

E

F

I

J

M

N

O

P

R

S

T

PowerPoint

A

B

C

D

S

T

U

V

W

Z

Publisher

A

B

C

D

F

G

T

U

V

W

Word

A

B

C

D

E

F

G

I

U

V

W